# Continuous Improvement in Higher Education

# Continuous Improvement in Higher Education

## How to Begin Your Institution's Lean Journey

Bonnie Slykhuis

**CRC Press**
Taylor & Francis Group
Boca Raton London New York

CRC Press is an imprint of the
Taylor & Francis Group, an **informa** business

A PRODUCTIVITY PRESS BOOK

First edition published in 2020
by Routledge/Productivity Press
52 Vanderbilt Avenue, 11th Floor New York, NY 10017

2 Park Square, Milton Park, Abingdon, Oxon OX14 4RN, UK
© 2020 by Bonnie Slykhuis

*Routledge/Productivity Press is an imprint of Taylor & Francis Group, an Informa business*

No claim to original U.S. Government works

Printed on acid-free paper

International Standard Book Number-13: 978-0-367-07666-5 (Paperback)

International Standard Book Number-13: 978-0-367-07668-9 (eBook)

International Standard Book Number-13: 978-0-367-40551-9 (Hardback)

---

**Library of Congress Cataloging-in-Publication Data**

---

LoC Data here

---

**Visit the Taylor & Francis web site at**
**www.taylorandfrancis.com**

This book is dedicated to my best friends and parents, Marvin and Patricia Slykhuis. You have instilled in me so many values including how to work hard, make work fun, how to dream big, work together, enjoy life, and value positive relationships. This book would not have been possible without those values or your endless love and support. Dad, I know you are still supporting me from heaven. Mom, you support me every day here on earth. Thank you for understanding all those weekends when I'd say "I have to go work on my book." We'd both laugh wondering if it would ever get done. Well mom, it did and now we can go play some more. Love you with all my heart.

Your loving daughter,
Bonnie

# Contents

# List of Tables and Figures

# Acknowledgments

I want to thank my dear friend and former Lean co-trainer, Janet Drake. You have been an invaluable person in the creation of this book and one of only a few people who actually knows what I'm talking about. Your eye for detail, your willingness to collaborate, your desire to educate, your passion for knowledge, and your willingness to dedicate time to help with this book can never be repaid. You are a true joy and here's to more adventures with you.

Steve Drake, you are a kind man whose opinion I value. Thank you for agreeing to be the non-content expert proofreader. Your insight and contributions are much appreciated.

Thank you to my long-time friend, author and junior high classmate Julie Marsh. It's destiny how our lives reconnected after many years and has aligned us on similar paths, to be authors. Thank you for your encouragement, support and enthusiasm for both writing and life. Doing this in parallel with you has been fun.

I want to thank my parents, Pat and Marvin Slykhuis; my siblings, Kim Molloy, Mike Slykhuis, Patrick Slykhuis, Dr. Jenny Slykhuis-McDowell, and Brian Slykhuis; my in-laws Lynn Slykhuis, Tina Slykhuis, Marty McDowell and Toni Slykhuis. Thank you all for the last 16 years of supporting and encouraging me whenever I talked about writing a book, which I'm sure you all thought would likely never happen.

# About the Author

**Bonnie Slykhuis** has had an interesting journey leading up to her current position as Lean/continuous improvement consultant for Des Moines Area Community College in Ankeny, Iowa.

Her journey as an instructor began with teaching middle school science and math along with coaching girls volleyball, basketball, track and softball in a small northwest Iowa community. Although she enjoyed teaching she yearned to pursue a career in the medical field. After becoming certified as an emergency medical technician she resigned her position and returned to college. Lack of financial resources forced her to quit after a year and move back to her hometown of Knoxville, Iowa. She worked part-time at Pella Corporation before landing full-time employment with 3M Company. During her 7 years at 3M she completed her Master's degree in Training and Development from Drake University, worked in production, was a member of the safety squad and served on a specialized team charged with designing and delivering training throughout the Knoxville plant.

During that time she often verbalized conditions of her ideal job which included working for a college, working with different companies, helping people to be better and being allowed to be creative. Having no knowledge that such a job existed she continued to look for new learning opportunities while searching for the ideal job. Deciding that working for different companies would improve her marketability she chose to accept a job with Maytag Corporation as a production supervisor in a union facility. Ten months later she was hired as a Lean trainer for Des Moines Area Community College (DMACC). The college had received a large Department of Labor grant to train manufacturing companies throughout Iowa on Lean tools and techniques. Bonnie became certified in value stream mapping, 5S, set-up reduction, cellular flow, Kanban, OSHA and later in several supervisory management training programs.

The ideal job she talked about was now hers. Her love of teaching, joy of problem-solving and knowledge of manufacturing had melded. In her years at DMACC, Bonnie has designed new programs to apply Lean to a variety of government, education, and service organizations. Her work in adapting and applying Lean within her college led to assisting other colleges across the country to begin building their own Lean program. Bonnie's understanding of the challenges facing higher education, recognition of the power Lean can have in helping meet those challenges, and realizing the lack of Lean training resources available to higher education led to her writing this book.

# Chapter 1

# Big Picture Rationale

Everyone knows that the world is changing. In fact, it is changing at a rate that surpasses any other time in our history. Fueled by innovation, global competition and technology, colleges and universities cannot afford to be complacent. They must find ways to adapt to current and future challenges or risk becoming obsolete like many companies (i.e. Kodak, Blockbuster, Palm, Toys-R-Us, General Mills, TWA) who were unwilling or slow to change.

The following are some of the impending challenges facing higher education. As you read through them consider whether your college is currently and effectively dealing with these challenges, whether they are planning to, or whether they need to do so.

- Funding – Colleges throughout the US continue to see a decline in state funding, forcing many to find ways to bridge the financial gap. According to a 2014 Government Accountability Office report, state funding for public colleges saw a 12% decline from 2003–2012 while the average tuition fee increased 55%.[1] The fluctuation in support is tied to the state's economy and competing demands for state funding with K-12 education, mental health coverage, Medicaid, and prisons to name a few. Based on these and other trends since 1980, the American Council in Education (ACE) predicts that "the average state fiscal support for higher education will reach zero by 2059."[2]
- Accountability of institutions – In the last decade student loans have jumped 150% leaving the average college/university graduate $25–50K in debt. The increased cost of higher education is forcing many to

consider options other than traditional advanced education after high school. To compound the problem, businesses are seeing a widening of the skills gap. Part of this is due to the pace of technology and the impact it has on the world we live in. Many of today's high-demand jobs didn't exist 10 years ago. Sixty-five percent of current grade school students will hold jobs that don't yet exist.[3] Much of the information that college students are currently learning will be obsolete by the time they graduate. Colleges/universities are struggling to keeping up with the ever changing demands of the workforce. To fill the skills gap companies must recruit from competitors or develop internal training programs. Colleges must find better ways to assess and align with current and future job needs or risk losing students due to poor job placement.

■ Competition for students – Students are no longer limited to regional colleges, physical campuses or standard class times. Through technology students can literally access classes around the world. Research continues to show a decline in traditional on-campus students while the numbers of online or distance learning students rise.[4] This and other shifts are forcing colleges to seek out new student populations (i.e. working adults, other countries) and evaluate how to better meet student needs (i.e. on-demand classes, shorter schedules, and adaptive teaching methods).[5] Some are turning to predictive analytics as a way to better target recruitment efforts and increase retention. The online news publication EdSurge reports that as the competition for traditional students tightens, the number of for-profit and non-profit college closures and acquisitions continues to trend upward.[6]

That brings us to talk about Lean, the subject of the next chapter. Lean is one way to effectively deal with many of the problems and issues facing institutions of higher education. My goal for this book is to narrow down the vast amounts of information about Lean into focused first steps that will hopefully aid you in setting up and starting your own Lean/continuous improvement program.

## Notes

1 Average tuition fees went from $3,745 in school year 2002–2003 to $5,800 in school year 2011–2012 for in-state students.

2 The ACE reported in State Funding: A Race to the Bottom (Mortensnson, 2012), that based on the trends since 1980, average state fiscal support for higher education will reach zero by 2059. Many reaching it by 2039.

3 https://www.youtube.com/watch?v=TwtS6Jy3ll8.

4 The Babson Research Group reported a 6.5% drop in students that study on US college campuses (1,173,805, or 6.4%) between 2012 and 2016 (Seaman, Allen, and Seaman, 2018).

5 A 2015 Changing Higher Education article reports that MIT is offering undergraduate courses online free of charge to students around the world. The online components will enable flexible time scales and location-independent participation.

6 According to the online news publication EdSurge, in the last two academic years, the number of nonprofit colleges decreased by nearly 2%. For-profit reductions were especially pronounced at 11%.

## Bibliography

Harris, A. 2018. Here's How Higher Education Dies. *The Atlantic*, (June) www.theatlantic.com/education/archive/2018/06/heres-how-higher-education-dies/561995/.

MIT's self-disruption: An update. October 13, 2015. *Changing Higher Education*. www.changinghighereducation.com/.

Mortenson, T. G. 2012. State Funding: A Race to the Bottom. American Council on Education. www.acenet.edu/the-presidency/columns-and-features/Pages/state-funding-a-race-to-the-bottom.aspx.

Seaman, J. E., Allen, I. E., and Seaman, J. 2018. Grade Increase: Tracking Distance Education in the United States, Babson Survey Research Group.

Seltzer, R. 2018. Moody's: Private-College Closures at 11 Per Year. *Inside Higher Education*, (July)www.insidehighered.com/news/2015/09/28/moodys-predicts-college-closures-triple-2017.

United States Government Accountability Office. 2014. Higher Education: State Funding Trends and Policies on Affordability. GAO-15-151. www.gao.gov/assets/670/667557.pdf.

# Chapter 2

---

# What Is Lean and Continuous Improvement?

---

When people hear the word *Lean* they often think of a reduction in staffing and doing more with less. Lean is not an acronym. It is a term that was first used by John Krafcik, an MIT graduate student, in an article he published in 1988. Jim Womack and Daniel Jones picked up the term and used it in their 1990 book, *The Machine That Changed The World*, making the word synonymous with process improvement. That book is about the car manufacturing industry and how the Japanese motor company, Toyota, designed a Lean production method that allowed them to produce and sell cars cheaper in the United States than American auto manufacturers. For more than 50 years Toyota has been achieving renowned success producing autos with nearly zero defects, developed efficiencies that have led to higher production, held the world's record for workplace appreciation and satisfaction, and many more notable accomplishments. The Toyota Production System, as it's known to many, has helped countless manufacturing companies throughout the world remain competitive and even thrive, because Toyota freely shared their methods and successes with the world. Seeing the successes in manufacturing, other business sectors such as healthcare, insurance, banking, software development, government, and education began modifying and adapting Toyota's model.

Many people do not realize that Lean is more than just a set of tools. It is a way of thinking, a way of behaving, and a set of tools.

- Way of thinking – Actively developing employee business and technical skills so they are able to make good decisions and be more productive. Training employees to continually identify wastes or inefficiencies and utilize problem-solving tools to remove inefficiencies from work processes.
- Way of behaving – Respecting one another and all departments, and a willingness to work together to solve problems. It involves actively soliciting ideas for improvement, encouraging teamwork, and helping co-workers to be their best.
- Set of tools – Tools provide the support structure and methods by which process improvement can happen. It's a systematic approach to evaluating, planning, and implementing change in order to achieve predictable outcomes. Used correctly the tools help identify underlying problems and their causes which can then be addressed versus guessing at solutions in the absence of Lean.

All of these are components of creating a Lean culture where maximum efficiency exists. Culture is not created overnight and Lean tools cannot solve all your problems. However, Lean can help strengthen your institution's ability to effectively meet many challenges that lie ahead.

Manufacturers see Lean as a critical part of doing business. More recently, colleges, universities, and other institutions of higher education around the world are also realizing the benefits of Lean, though they may refer to it by another name. Whether you call it Lean, process improvement, continuous improvement, rapid process improvement, kaizen or another term is not important. What is important is that your institution understands the level of commitment needed, and the potential benefits that can be gained in order to make a decision on whether or not to start a formal Lean/continuous improvement program.

Below are three working definitions that we will utilize throughout the rest of this book.

1. *Lean* – A fundamental approach that teaches people to first see waste and then use various tools to remove the waste from work activities (such as processes and work spaces). All employees work together to make positive change.
2. *Process improvement* – Improvements that focus on work processes, as opposed to organizing workspaces, strategic planning, or solving a specific problem. Usually involves mapping of processes.

3. *Continuous improvement* – On-going, continuous re-evaluation of all work activities to make incremental improvements over a long period of time.

## 2.1 Underlying Problems

Take a moment and think about where you want your institution to be in the next 5 to 10 years. What challenges lie ahead of you and how can you get your institution in shape to effectively meet those challenges? Athletes don't show up for competition on day one and expect to do well. They know they have to work on getting their body in shape, practice every day, and hone in on eliminating specific performance weaknesses. Think of your institution as an athlete getting ready for competition. As you prepare to meet the challenges ahead, what weaknesses and underlying issues do you need to start working on to ensure you are ready for competition? Athletes often spend hours working on improving one tiny skill that can give them that slight competitive edge over their opponent. It might be foot placement, a step, a swing, a grip, or a follow-through. Something that only the athlete is conscious of.

What are your institutional weaknesses? Those underlying problems that could hinder your institution's ability to remain competitive in the future? The following assessment (Table 2.1 Assessment of Institutional Challenges/Problems) is intended to help your institution identify what underlying issues it may have that could cause significant problems or even derailment if not properly addressed. A strong Lean/continuous improvement program could help with many of these by providing the structure and momentum for change. Try answering the questions from your institution's perspective. If needed, narrow the focus to what you have knowledge of (i.e. college, campus, department, or site). Circle the response for each question that most clearly matches your institution's current status.

Count the number of responses in each column and multiply it by the score designated at the top (1, 5 and 10). This should give you an indication of your institution's need for a continuous improvement program. For example, if most of your circled answers fall in the right-hand column (score above 70) your institution has a lot of opportunity and could benefit from such a program, assuming you have the right leadership support.

**Table 2.1   Assessment of Institutional Challenges/Problems**

| Questions | Score=1 | Score =5 | Score=10 |
|---|---|---|---|
| Funding trend over the last 5 years | Increasing | Same | Decreasing |
| Enrollment trends over the last 5 years | Increasing | Same | Decreasing |
| Budget constraints over past 5 years | Decreasing | Same | Increasing |
| Leaders share a common vision | Yes | Some | No |
| Department goals align with institutional strategic goals | Directly align | Some alignment | No clear alignment |
| Expectations have been established and documented for departments and staff positions | Yes | Sometimes | Rarely or never |
| There is clear communication of performance expectations for staff and departments | Yes | Sometimes | Rarely or never |
| Consistency of policies and procedures across locations/ departments | Consistent | Some | Inconsistent |
| Level of trust among employees | High | Medium | Low |
| Level of collaboration between departments | Frequent | Some | Minimal |
| Employee attitude towards change | Proactive | Reactive | Avoidance |
| Majority of work processes/ procedures are: | Documented | Some documented | Undocumented |
| Format of majority of work processes are: | Electronic | 50/50 | Paper |
| A program exists within the institution to evaluate process efficiency with stakeholders | Yes | Some | No |

*(Continued)*

**Table 2.1 (Cont.)**

| Questions | Score=1 | Score =5 | Score=10 |
|---|---|---|---|
| Leadership behaviors towards continuous improvement | Promote | Indifferent | Discourage |
| Level to which leadership actively promotes problem-solving | Frequently | Sometimes | Rarely |
| Employee involvement in skill development activities/trainings within the college (excluding conferences) | Frequent | Sometimes | Rarely |
| Level of involvement of front-line staff in designing changes | Frequent | Sometimes | Rarely |
| Extent to which personnel performance problems are addressed | Timely | Varies | Rarely |
| Employee reporting of process problems (errors, delays, barriers) | Openly/ timely | Occasionally | Not encouraged |
| Total Counts | | | |

# Reference

Womack J.P., Jones D.T. and Ross D. 1990. *The Machine that Changed the World.* New York: Rawson Associates.

# *Chapter 3*

---

# What Is Waste?

---

In our society we have lean products (lean ground beef, Lean Cuisine, lean whey products) that have had the fat and/or excess calories removed from them because some customers do not want the full-fat version. Lean in our work activities is much the same. It's about removing the excess steps (fat) that prevent a company or an institution from being efficient. It's also those things or activities for which, if given a choice, customers would be unwilling to pay. We call these *wastes* or *non-value-added activities*. Lean focuses on using tools and step-by-step methods to remove waste from work processes so information and/or product *flows* more efficiently throughout a process.

All work activities can be sorted into two basic categories, value-added (VA) and non-value-added (NVA). VA steps are necessary to provide a product or service. We determine VA steps based on their value to the customer. These include both internal and external customers. If, given a choice, the customer would be willing to pay for these steps if they could see the whole process. These steps create value for them.

An example of VA steps in higher education relating to student admissions is students filling out an application with required information and submitting it to admissions. Additional VA would be for the admissions department to review the application for completeness and eligibility before processing it in the system. The system would then generate communications back to the students informing them of their status. Each of these steps are essential for admitting a student to the college/university and keeping them informed of their admission status.

NVA, on the other hand, are those steps that create no value in the process. Also called wastes, these activities consume valuable time, money, personnel, and materials. If, given a choice, customers would not be willing to pay for these steps or activities. Staying with the example of students submitting an application for admission, non-value added steps would include receiving a paper application from a student and having to re-type the information into an electronic system, manually re-formatting or re-verifying addresses, searching or calling for missing information, rechecking the same information multiple times, printing and filing copies of documents that no one will use, and sending redundant communications.

Let's use another example to show NVA work. Imagine your department or workgroup is holding a big meeting. Someone is assigned to make the big pot of coffee for the group. In this example, the person assigned the job to make the coffee does not drink coffee nor have they been trained, much like a new employee trying to figure out work tasks without being properly trained or having access to work instructions. If we were to observe this person and document their steps, Figure 3.1 shows what we might see.

In looking at the steps, how long would it take this person to make coffee compared to someone who drinks and makes coffee regularly (the experienced employee)? Likely much more time. Next question, what is the quality

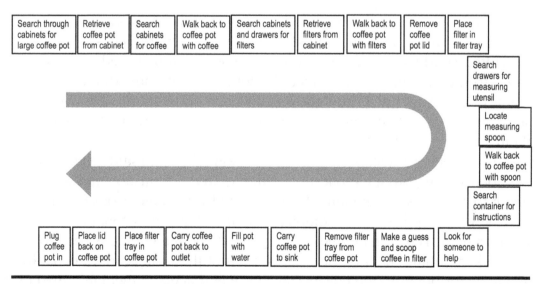

**Figure 3.1   Mapping the Process**

expectation? Can the group be guaranteed a good cup of coffee? Probably not. In the case of Lean, we would use the process mapping tool to map out all the steps in the process and then evaluate each of those steps to determine their value to the customer. Take for example, the first step of looking through the cabinets for the large coffee pot. As a customer would you be willing to pay for someone to search for things? Imagine going to Starbucks when you are in a hurry. Would you continue going there if each time you ordered coffee you had to wait for the worker to go searching for cups, coffee, and other essential items? How would this impact the number of customers they could serve in a day? How would their business be affected? NVA steps delay service to the customer, create extra work that costs money, and diminishes the quality. Figure 3.2 below shows the NVA steps shaded. In truth, these shaded steps are not essential to making coffee. So how do we get rid of these "wasteful" steps?

Once waste has been identified it's time to find solutions to reduce or eliminate it. In our coffee example many of you would apply common sense to the situation and, with a little added creativity, your final results would likely consist of basic Lean tools such as placing supplies near where the work is being done. We call this *point of use storage.* Creating simple visual work instructions on how to make the coffee is an example of *standard work.* Standard work is the most efficient method to produce a product (or perform a service) to achieve a desired output. It breaks down the work into

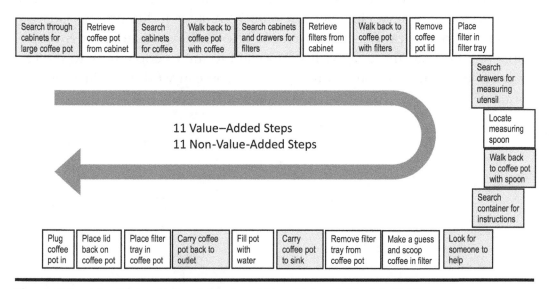

**Figure 3.2   Identifying Value-Added and Non-Value-Added Activities**

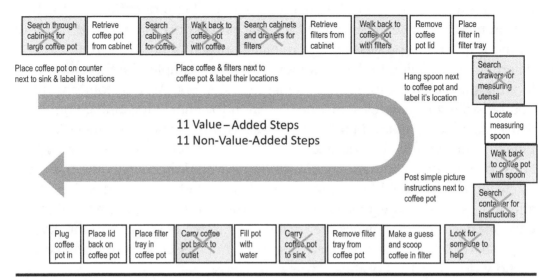

**Figure 3.3    Improvements to Reduce Non-Value-Added Activities**

elements, which are sequenced, organized, and can repeatedly be followed. Pictures of how to make the coffee and labeling where items are to be stored are both examples of *visual controls* – simple visual signals or displays that provide instructions. Upon implementation of these improvement ideas (Figure 3.3), could you predict that a new person could make the coffee more quickly? Would they be more likely to ensure a good cup of coffee? The only true way to know is to test it, but in this instance the likelihood is pretty high since we've eliminated several NVA steps in the process.

The goal of any process improvement is to remove waste in order to improve efficiency and quality. It's important to train people how to recognize waste, because if you can recognize it, you can work to reduce or eliminate it.

# Chapter 4

## Common Types of Waste

Training everyone how to recognize waste is the foundation to building your Lean culture. It provides a common vocabulary and if people can see the waste around them they can start taking steps to reduce or eliminate it. If you search the internet for Lean wastes you will find standard lists of seven to eight common types of work wastes. I have added a ninth waste (confusion) only because I find it to be prevalent in every work environment and I don't feel that it is adequately captured within the other wastes. The lists of wastes may be ordered differently or use slightly different wording but the types, with the exception of *confusion*, remain consistent and are listed below.

## 4.1 Defects and Errors

This waste occurs anytime you receive something that is incomplete, inaccurate, or missing, which prevents you from completing your work steps until the problem is corrected. How much time do you or your staff spend fixing things that are not correct or gathering missing information? I once worked with a college admissions group who was trying to reduce processing time for student applications. To speed up the process they launched an online application. Unfortunately, the online form contained several free-format data fields, meaning anything could be typed into them. In reviewing the process it was calculated that 70% of the applications they received had to be edited just to fix the address errors for things such as all capital letters, all small letters, incorrect abbreviations and invalid addresses. Standardized formatting and accuracy were important because these same addresses

16

would later download directly from the student information system (SIS) to send communications to students. To eliminate the error the department installed previously purchased software (it was sitting on the shelf but never utilized) that validated addresses with the post office and formatted them as well. They also programmed error-proofing measures into the online application such as allowing students to select from a drop-down menu versus typing in information, requiring specific formats for emails and phone numbers, identifying required fields, and inserting links or pop-ups to further clarify the information being requested. By eliminating these and other application errors the college was able to reduce the average processing time for applications from 26.3 days to 1.4, which freed up staff to do other work.

If your college or department is still reliant on paper forms, defects and error waste will exist. People can write anything they want in the fields on paper forms or even leave them blank. Online forms can provide an array of error-proofing measures for all types of processes by utilizing drop-down menus, required fields (must complete to continue), required formatting (answer must be in the form of an email, phone numbers, etc.), conditional formatting (depending on how you answer a question, additional questions might appear), and automated workflows (auto-routing of forms to the next person or task).

Causes of defects and errors include:

- Lack of standard work – everyone is doing the task differently
- Lack of documented work processes
- Unclear requests – person is not sure what is needed or what is being asked for
- Outdated forms
- Redundant data entry – systems that don't talk to each other so information has to be re-entered, increasing chances for errors
- Lack of training on standard procedures
- Paper processes

## 4.2 Overprocessing

Overprocessing is caused by doing more than is necessary from the customer's viewpoint. Sometimes this waste is caused just by failing to review processes from time to time and determining what's really needed or essential. Have you ever asked why something was done a certain way only to be told, "Because we've always done it that way"? Things are always changing, so just because you made three carbon copies of a particular form on different colored paper years ago or created and distributed those monthly green-bar reports to department leaders in the past, it doesn't mean that's what should be done today.

Several years ago as part of a Lean project, I was working with three different departments within a college on an invoicing process for contract training services which two of the departments provided to external business clients. At the time, each department had their own process for sending invoices to clients and following up on payments. To add to the over-processing, one department had a process in which they created the invoice on the computer, tore apart a triplicate invoice template (pink, yellow, green), loaded those same sheets into the printer, and printed the colored copies. The yellow copy was placed in the department file, pink was sent to the business office and green was sent to human resources (HR). Each department was asked why their copy was needed, what they did with it and if the color was important. Since HR was not a part of the Lean project a person was assigned to find out what they did with their invoice copy. When asked, HR personnel said they shredded it. For more than 15 years they had been shredding all the contract training invoices received from that department because they had no use for it. Did anyone from HR ever call to say, "Stop sending us these invoices"? In all that time, HR did not call even once to say they didn't need the invoices. Nor did the originating department ever call to see if the other departments still needed their copies. Why? "Because that's how it's always been done." I strongly urge you to question everything. Don't be afraid to ask, "Is this really necessary?" because you might find that it's not or that there is a better way to do it.

Another example of waste from overprocessing is having to enter the same information multiple times in different locations. If you have technology systems that don't communicate, causing you to re-enter information from one system into another system, you are duplicating work. Or perhaps you have processes that require students to fill out a series of forms based on their program of study. How many different times do we require them to re-write their name, student number, email, etc.? I recall a doctor's visit in which I had to write my name, birthdate, and phone number ten different times for the various forms. When I returned three months later for a follow-up, I had to fill all the forms out again because it was a new year. How many times did the person in the doctor's office have to re-enter my name, address, and phone number for all those forms?

Ideally I should have had to provide it once, or better yet, simply validate that the information in their system was correct.

Not knowing what others are doing in a process also creates waste from overprocessing. A multi-campus college was reviewing their admissions process. In doing so, they discovered that the satellite campuses were able to process a portion of student applications but then would forward them by mail to the main campus to be completed. The main campus admissions staff, not knowing that parts of the applications were already reviewed and verified, reprocessed the entire application, duplicating those parts that had already been done. The main campus ended up providing training to the satellite campuses so they could complete the entire processing of applications for students attending their campus, thus sharing the workload.

Another classic example of overprocessing that I have to mention, because it is so common, is the use of Excel spreadsheets. Spreadsheets are great for keeping track of information and the ability to calculate and sort information. However, it becomes a problem when there is not a common spreadsheet that everyone can access. I once used the Lean tool of process mapping to review a payroll process in which each department tracked their employees' time on a separate spreadsheet. Part of the problem was that each department had created their own spreadsheet so each one was different from the next. To add to the overprocessing problem each department printed their spreadsheet at the end of each pay period, routed it for signatures then hand-delivered it to the payroll clerk in another building. More overprocessing occurred when the payroll clerk had to sort all the spreadsheets and then manually enter each employee's time into the payroll system. The process was changed to allow employees to electronically enter and submit timesheets which were then electronically routed for approval and easily processed by the payroll clerk eliminating all spreadsheets, printed copies, and data re-entry!

Causes of overprocessing include:

- Lack of standard procedures
- Lack of training to standard procedures
- Lack of knowledge about the process – what happens upstream and downstream
- Multiple technology systems that don't talk to each other – causing redundant data entry

■ Inadequate tools/knowledge of the job – leading to creation of work arounds to find alternative and often lengthy ways to complete the job
■ Unclear customer requests or expectations

## 4.3 Waiting

Waiting is caused when you fail to have *what* you need to do your task, not having what is needed *when* you need it, and not having what is needed in the format or condition you need it to complete your tasks. For example, the information or item might be incomplete, defective, or require extra processing. Waiting can be caused by internal customers, external customers, or systems. Hiring processes are commonly plagued with waiting. Hiring departments wait on leaders to approve positions. Departments wait on HR to post the jobs. HR waits for job postings to close. Departments wait on HR to pre-screen and release applicants. HR waits on departments to screen, interview, and select candidates. Candidates wait to hear about hiring status. HR waits on background checks. Departments wait for the new hire to start. All of this becomes even slower if you are still relying on paper to be passed around between departments.

One of the most frequent forms of waiting I see when reviewing processes is waiting for approvals/signatures. I once reviewed a hiring process for a large state university. Their typical lead time from request for the position by a department to the position being filled was six months. Much of their waiting was due to the lack of complete and accurate information about the position in the very beginning of the process. During the process, position information was manually routed (paper) to the different departments for approval. Frequently the request would get sent back for corrections or amendments due to missing or incomplete information. Each time the request was sent back it caused the process to start over. To add to the waiting, there were multiple approvers in the process. If approvers were out of the office, the requests had to wait for their return. In addition, if one approver made changes the whole process started over once again. In this situation, the university improved the process by implementing a pre-hire planning tool/process. It ensured that the most complete and accurate information was assembled before the hiring process started. They also cut the number of approvers by half, reduced the number of steps by approximately 38% and automated many of them.

Causes of waiting:

■ Unclear requests for information
■ Lack of planning
■ Lack of standard processes and timelines
■ Information gate keepers – limited number of people with information who may choose not to share the information to retain power and control
■ Lack of technology – manual routing of paper, delayed responses
■ Slow/unreliable systems
■ Errors and rework

## 4.4 Overproduction

Colleges and universities do not make products but we still over produce. How often do you or people in your department make copies that go in a file? Do you know that between 50–80% of things that get filed never get accessed again (Dubkinsky, 2012)? I see this repeatedly in my work in office settings. Many of us make paper copies of things because we don't trust our electronic systems or "we've always done it that way." I worked with a department in a higher educational institution to document their contract training and grant funded training processes which were used to provide training to external clients. In mapping the process they discovered that their department was unknowingly creating 27 copies of the same training contract. Each person that touched the document made a personal copy for their file before passing it to the next person in the process. This included the administrative assistant who did nothing other than receive the document, make a copy and send it to the next person in line. What did this create? Excessive copies filling up filing cabinets, excess materials being consumed, added staff time to print and file the documents, and wasted time searching for the "official" document. Why did this happen? People involved in the process didn't trust the system nor did they understand all the steps in the process, which is quite common. Plus, they were used to a paper process where everyone had their own working files. Shortly after the problem was realized the department implemented a SharePoint document management system reducing the number of copies from 27 to 1 and implemented electronic workflows, which reduced contract approval time from 48 hours to 2 hours.

Another area in which we often see waste from overproduction is marketing. Marketing departments, printing departments, and those departments using their services are notorious for producing more than is needed. Why? Because the more you order the cheaper it is and the mind-set is that it's better to have excess than run out. As an example of overproduction, I recall a project I led in which we evaluated the creation and distribution of the course catalogs which marketed the class schedules for the upcoming semester. Catalogs were mailed to current and potential students but copies were also made available at the various campuses and centers. By reviewing the process the college was able to reduce printing costs by $16,000 simply by asking each location how many catalogs they needed based on past history.

Causes of overproduction:

- Producing just in case we need it
- Unclear document retention standards/expectations
- Lack of knowledge about the process
- Failure to evaluate what's needed – old vs. new practices
- Unclear requests or expectations – printing hand-outs that nobody uses

## 4.5 Excess Inventory

If you are reading this at work take a moment right now and count the number of writing utensils (pens, pencils, and markers) you currently have in your workspace. Look in your drawers, under your stacks of materials and anywhere else you might have them stashed. If you are like most people, you probably have somewhere between 15 and 30 writing utensils in your immediate workspace. Now, how many pens/pencils do you use on a regular basis? The normal answer I receive is two to four. Why do you have so many if you only use two to four? Already I can hear you trying to justify the numbers: people take them, I pick them up at conferences, I can't find them when I need them, and the list goes on. If you generally use three pens/pencils that means anything more than that is excess inventory. We are just talking about writing utensils. What else do you have stashed or stored that isn't needed or you have in excess? How many things do you have in your workspaces that are not essential to your work or do not belong in your workspace?

Excess inventory is defined as anything that is unneeded or having more than is needed for a reasonable amount of time. For example, if you have files you've never accessed (and are not required to keep) you have excess inventory. If you haven't purged your space of unneeded items in the last year you have excess inventory. Excess inventory creates clutter and causes inefficiency. The average American worker spends at least an hour a day searching for things lost in clutter.[1] It doesn't matter if it's physical stuff or electronic information stored in shared drives or email folders, the more stuff you accumulate, the more time is wasted, and the more stress you experience. Every office has excess inventory and that amount grows when retention standards do not exist, are not communicated, are not followed, and are not practiced regularly.

On a continuum most offices exist somewhere between having paper-driven processes and electronic (paperless) processes. As a result, documents are often duplicated, existing both electronically and on paper. When working with offices to map work steps I often hear, "I copy the document, then file it." Each time I hear that phrase I proceed with a series of questions:

*Me:* "Why do you copy it?"
*Worker:* "So I can put it in my file"
*Me:* "Why do you put it in your file?"
*Worker:* "In case someone asks for it."
*Me:* "How many times in the last month have you been asked for it or referenced it?"

The common answer I get – "None or once." Of course this depends on the situation.

My next question, "What is the worst thing that would happen if you didn't have it in the file?"
*Worker:* "I would tell them I don't know or I'd look the information up in the system."

So in short, this person is copying and filing multiple documents a day that are rarely or never accessed, which in turn costs the workplace money, time, space, and materials for something that is already stored electronically.

Let's consider other examples of excess inventory. I have worked with numerous campuses, departments, and programs, ranging from healthcare, culinary arts, technology, automotive, marketing, childcare, and various work trades, all seeking help to organize labs, storerooms, cabinets, offices, and vehicles. Each event exposed the vast inefficiency of excess inventory which consumes valuable workspace and increases the time spent hunting for items. When I do a project pre-assessment, which is basically a walk-through to determine the scope of a project, I am not shy about opening cabinets, drawers, toolboxes, and closets to see how space is being used. In the vast majority of cases, it's not the space that's the issue, it's how the space is being utilized. Excess inventory leads to a whole lot of NVA activity, such as extra handling of items, damaged/defective items, and excess motion searching for and moving things.

Let me ask, do you have a junk drawer, junk room, or junk garage at home? Almost everyone does. It's that place where you stash stuff when you don't know where it goes or you don't take the time to put it in its proper location. How often do you look for things in that space? How often do you find what you're looking for? How much time do you spend searching? And, what happens when you don't find what you're looking for within a reasonable amount of time? You go buy more, right? Then you throw that in the "junk storage" and the problem continues.

Each time I lead a 5S (Lean tool used to organize workspaces) event with a group, I wait for five things to take place. One, they find something they've been looking for but haven't been able to locate for a period of time. Two, they find something of historical value and usually comment with something like "I can't believe I still have this" or "Why in the world would anyone have kept this." Three, they find something of comical value like a past college president's fish photo, a bread recipe from someone who can't cook or a cheesy vacation souvenir that once doubled as some sort of traveling trophy. Four, they find multiples of items of which they were certain they only had one or two. Five, they find items that are outdated, obsolete, or expired and can no longer be used such as medical supplies, batteries, technology, media, and other items. Excess inventory not only increases costs associated with materials, space, and worker time but also increases worker anxiety and frustration related to searching for needed items, which negatively impacts productivity.

Causes of excess inventory:

■ Lack of retention standards or lack of awareness of retention standards
■ Lack of trust in the process, other people, or the system – e.g. everyone has their own "stash" of supplies, documents, information
■ Lack of organizational skills and training
■ Lack of a system or process for purging excess items

- Failure to establish minimum and maximum inventory limits on items – e.g. when down to one ink cartridge, order only two more cartridges
- Lack of awareness on what's needed and how much

## 4.6 Unnecessary Transport

Unnecessary transport occurs when you are moving people, information, or things from place to place without adding value to the product or service. Take for example paper forms and documents that get sent through inter-campus or postal mail to other locations. How much time does it spend in transit, getting sorted, delivered, and just sitting at the different staging areas without anything of value happening to it? An example of this process can be viewed on my YouTube channel.[2] In the video, a paper document requiring just two signatures travels from one end of a campus to the other, totaling 61 steps, 12 handoffs, 24 hours, and 2.4 miles. What is it the customer wants or needs? They need two approval signatures. We can even question if both signatures are really needed. The rest of the steps are NVA. Now, how could you eliminate the documents just traveling around? Make them electronic. Using the right system, the processing or approval time could be reduced from days and hours to literally minutes. The same goes for employees traveling to meetings vs. holding webinars or conference calls. I realize some meetings require face-to-face, but which ones do not?

Causes of unnecessary transport:

- Paper processes
- Lack of good technology solutions
- Poor work area layout
- Lack of training on available technology
- Centralized receiving – e.g. when one campus receives and then must redistribute materials to other campuses

## 4.7 Excess Motion

Excess motion differs from excess transportation in that it focuses more on your personal workspace and the motions you go through to do your job. It occurs when you fail to have items/information where you need it, when you need it and how you need it. Remember the coffee example from earlier? The new person making coffee spent time searching and retrieving the needed items. It's the same with your physical or electronic work spaces. Consider the number of steps you take or clicks you go through to find the documents or materials you need most often. Think about this. When you first got hired into your job, did you replace someone? If so, chances are you inherited their stuff *and* their set up. You were probably reluctant to throw things away because you didn't know if you needed them or not. Then, once you learned the job, you probably didn't take, or have, time to go back through and clean out, right? So imagine if I asked you to take everything out of your workspace and sort out only the stuff you needed plus a few personal items. Next, I asked you to think about your workflow and to strategically put those items back in the most efficient locations based on how frequently you used them and taking into consideration your workflow. Things you use most often should be the easiest to access and closest to you. The less you use items the farther away they should be located. If you did these things, would you put everything back in your space exactly the way it is right now? Likely not. Think of how much time you and others spend sorting, searching, moving, touching information and items without adding value to them. Ideally, if you touch it you should add value to it. If you don't add value, it's likely you have excess motion. This also applies to accessing information in electronic format. How many clicks must you go through to find and retrieve documents, files, or information? Quick menus, search features, standard naming conventions and organized file/folder structures can help reduce excess motion.

Causes of excess motion:

- Poor organizational skills and practices
- Lack of standard procedures
- Lack of training (technology and process)
- Lack of designated space to store items
- Systems that do not communicate or work together
- Lack of a document management system
- Errors and rework, overproduction, overprocessing, excess inventory

## 4.8 Under-Utilized People

Under-utilization of people occurs when you fail to use people's skills and abilities to their fullest potential. It might also be referred to as lack of employee engagement. Most people want to be allowed to do their jobs to the best of their abilities. Unfortunately, they often encounter barriers preventing them from achieving that desire. Barriers include: not having the right equipment or tools for the job, limited authority to do their job, unhealthy work environments, lack of training, and lack of opportunity to perform at their best.

Many years ago I resigned as a middle school math and science teacher to go back to school to pursue a career in the health sciences. I landed a part-time job as a lab assistant in an immunology research lab at a large university. Since my bachelor's degree was in biology, I was excited about the job and the opportunity to learn. It didn't take long to realize this wasn't the place for me. The environment was oppressive and as a lab assistant I was given strict instructions to "not touch or do anything unless specifically told." This went totally against my upbringing where I was taught to take initiative, do what needs to be done and do a good job. Unfortunately, the environment mirrored that of the head research doctor who was routinely rude and condescending to everyone in the lab. Ironically, the lab lost its funding shortly after I started and I was glad to seek other employment. The climate he established is what is referred to as a control and command environment. One in which employees are taught and conditioned to do only what they are told and not to ask questions. Not only were employees not engaged but it was also a hostile work environment, both of which negatively impact productivity. As you work to build your Lean structure and ultimately your Lean culture, consider methods to encourage and recognize employee involvement, knowledge, skills, and contributions.

Causes of under-utilized people:

- Culture of control and command
- Lack of trust
- Lack of appropriate tools for the job
- Unclear expectations
- Lack of training
- Inefficient processes
- Lack of opportunity for employees to do their best
- Broken, inefficient processes
- Lack of respect

## 4.9 Confusion

Confusion is a waste you will not see in any internet searches for types of work wastes. This is a waste that I have personally added because I see this as being very prevalent in most work environments. I define confusion as any instance in which you are uncertain of the next course of action. Confusion can lead to all of the other wastes we've already talked about. In every process that I have reviewed or helped review I have observed people trying hard to do the best job they can. I believe that no one tries to do a bad job on purpose unless they are motivated to do so. Unfortunately, bad processes make even the best workers look bad. Let's look at a simple task I observed while teaching a Lean class at a community college. I had just called for a short break when I watched several people from the class get up to exit the room. On their way out of the room they wanted to properly dispose of their soda cans, bottles and other garbage. What you see in Figure 4.1 is what was located in back of the room. Do

**Figure 4.1   Confusion**

you see a problem? I watched as students struggled with this very simple task of trying to dispose of their garbage properly. They were trying to do the right thing. I watched as some dropped their cans or bottle in the container on the left. After doing so they saw the sign on the right. Other actions I observed included:

- Removing their can/bottle from the left container and depositing it in the right container
- Removing their can/bottle from the right container and depositing it in the left container
- Trying to switch the lids which failed because the containers were different sizes
- Leaving the can/bottle in the left-hand container
- Leaving the can/bottle in the right-hand container
- Not being sure what was correct so leaving their can/bottle on the floor

So who is right in this situation? Everyone was trying to do the right thing and dispose of their trash properly. However, because of their confusion more work was created for the next person in the process, the building custodian. If this simple problem isn't corrected, it's quite possible the custodian will be left with a bad perception of students and their abilities to properly dispose of trash items. Broken or confusing processes make both workers and customers look bad. They can lead to negative assumptions about people's abilities to do the job and many other wastes. Ironically, in this situation of students trying to properly dispose of their trash, Figure 4.2 shows the clearly labeled containers that were right down the hall.

Causes of confusion:

- Lack of standards
- Lack of training
- Lack of clear visual controls or visual instructions
- Failure to follow standard procedures
- Unclear requests for work
- Unclear expectations

In summation, I believe it's important to educate employees at all levels about the common types of work wastes. It's not as important to remember the names of each type of waste as it is to develop the ability to recognize them. Recognizing them allows everyone an opportunity to begin reducing or

**Figure 4.2  Non-Confusion**

removing them. Learning about the wastes also provides common terminology which everyone understands and can use in improvement discussions.

Hopefully by now you have a better understanding of the types of wastes and why recognizing them is so important to starting one's Lean journey. It's likely that as you read through the descriptions of wastes you recognized a plethora of opportunities for improvement at your institution. It might even seem a bit overwhelming and confusing about where to start. The important thing is that you do get started, so on to the next chapter where we discuss tools for removing waste.

## Notes

1  www.cottrillresearch.com/various-survey-statistics-workers-spend-too-much-time-searching-for-information/
2  www.youtube.com/watch?v=ghHzhI29wYc

## Reference

Dubkinsky, D. 2012. *Surprising Stats, Simply Orderly*. http://www.simplyorderly.com/surprising-statistics/.

# Chapter 5

# Lean Tools

What is a tool? A tool is a something used to aid one in completing a task. A hammer is a tool to help drive a nail and a broom is a tool to help clean the floor. Tools make the job easier, but it's important to select the right tool for each job. You can use pliers, a socket wrench, or crescent wrench to turn a bolt, but finding the best solution depends upon the task and what you are trying to achieve. You may also find that multiple tools can be used together to complete a task and that some tools are more complex than others. For example, a high-speed power drill with a socket is better suited for certain jobs than a single wrench.

Lean tools serve the same purpose and are similar to tools in a tool box. There are simple Lean tools such as visual controls (e.g. color-coding, lines, signs, labels, and pictures) which, when applied to work-spaces, make it easier to locate items more quickly. There are also more complex tools like value-stream mapping, process mapping, and 5S that guide you step-by-step through improving work processes and work spaces. Lean tools help create efficiencies by solving problems and reducing waste. They help make the tasks of fixing problems and processes easier and more efficient.

Consider for a moment how problems are commonly addressed in an environment where Lean methodologies or tools are not used. Let's assume that a sizeable problem occurs and is reported in a staff meeting. The person sharing the information provides their perspective of the problem and offers educated guesses about the cause. Normal behavior then follows where individuals begins brainstorming possible solutions. In the absence of Lean, personalities determine solutions. If there are several people in the room, whose solution is likely to get adopted? Chances are it's either the senior person in charge or the strongest personality, otherwise known as the most vocal. The other participants, accustomed to the likely outcomes, frequently elect to withhold their ideas. So the "chosen" solution is acted upon without fully knowing the scope of the issue, how it affects other areas and with little to no vetting of other potential solutions. The chosen idea is implemented, but the results often fall short of expectations, or worse yet, create problems elsewhere. It's like the game of whack-a-mole in the old arcades. You whack one mole on the head and another immediately pops up somewhere else. This type of approach to problem-solving is also referred to as the shotgun approach, because with a shotgun cartridge the shot in the ammo cartridge scatters in all directions with many missing the target. The overall success rate can be pretty low. Without Lean it manifests as picking random solutions to fix a problem without understanding how they are all connected.

Let's imagine you've selected payroll processing as a top priority during your leadership session. All that is currently known is that payroll is continuing to have problems getting adjuncts paid correctly and getting payroll processed in a timely manner. There have also been a few times when employee paychecks have been delayed, causing all sorts of other issues. Without having a method to dive into the process, there might be a tendency to jump to quick assumptions, solutions, and place blame on staff or departments such as those listed below.

- Payroll isn't working hard enough to submit payroll on time – so remind them of the deadline. *As if they don't already know the deadline and its importance.*
- Payroll needs more people to process payroll – see if we can find additional help. *This is just covering up the underlying wastes that are occurring.*
- Department administrative assistants are failing to process adjunct paperwork correctly causing incorrect payment of adjuncts – so we need to retrain them. *Training might be an issue but likely additional problems are a factor.*
- Supervisors are not approving time correctly – we need to re-emphasize the importance of correctly approving time and maybe do training. *If multiple supervisors are not approving time correctly that should be a red flag that something is amiss, perhaps confusion, lack of standards, and other wastes.*

Without the use of a Lean-mapping tool (described later in this chapter) to evaluate the payroll process, the actions to address these assumptions would likely have nothing to do with the real problem. If the wrong action were taken it could even affect worker morale.

I stated earlier that broken processes make even the best workers look bad. The scenarios above were real and taken from actual Lean projects I have led. In the case of adjuncts not getting paid correctly, the administrative assistant in the department was initially reprimanded. Later, when the process was reviewed, it was discovered that the college Dean had not established expectations regarding submission of adjunct paperwork nor communicated deadlines about pay schedules. In addition, the hiring supervisor under the Dean failed to correctly complete the hiring paperwork and submit it in time to be processed prior to the first pay date. One of the new adjuncts, assuming she should have received a paycheck on the first pay date, yelled at the administrative assistant. If the hiring paperwork had been submitted on time and the pay schedule had been correctly and clearly communicated, the new adjunct would have been informed that, based on her teaching assignment, she would receive pay on the second pay date rather than the first. If you were the administrative assistant in this scenario how would you be feeling about now? Also, what impression might the new adjunct have about their new employer?

The other payroll scenarios in these preceding examples (i.e. supervisors incorrectly approving time, delays in payroll processing) were common problems until the college decided to evaluate the process using process mapping described later in this chapter. The mapping event revealed a great deal of confusion around the types of acceptable leaves for the different pay classifications (part-time, full-time, hourly, salaried, salaried non-exempt, etc.). For example, things like "exempt salaried staff can only take leave in whole or half days," but "hourly full-time staff can take leave in hour increments." There were no system checks in place and many supervisors were unsure what to check for. This resulted in multiple leave time errors getting passed through the system until they arrived in the payroll office. The payroll staff would work long hours on pay weeks to clean up the mistakes in time for the bank transaction on Friday.

As you can see, a problem can have many underlying issues. Mapping the process can help uncover most of those compounding issues in a systematic way leading to better and more predictable improvements.

In the next chapter we will discuss the importance of doing your research. I urge you to go see what others are doing and participate in Lean classes and events. Learn about various Lean tools and how they are being used. Expose yourself to different methods of conducting process improvement. Look for those things that are simple, effective and likely to fit with your institution. If you've hired someone with a strong background in Lean, they will likely drive what tools and approaches you use. But, if you have a less experienced team leading your charge, it's not uncommon to feel a bit overwhelmed and confused about which approach and tools to use to start your program.

As a Lean practitioner having worked in a variety of businesses, industries, governments, and college/university settings for nearly two decades, I'm going to advise you on the simplest, most fundamental tools that will help you address 75% of your problems. These two tools are simple, intuitive and something everyone in your organization can learn to use. These tools are *process mapping* and *5S*, both of which are described in this chapter. They are my "go-to" tools which I still use for most of the projects I do. Their fundamental elements can be applied and adapted to a variety of situations. Make it easy on yourself. Get really good at these two tools and then you can always add more tools to your toolbox as the need arises.

## 5.1 Mapping Tools

You've already heard me mention mapping tools several times. Much of what you will be looking at within your college has to do with processes. Colleges and universities have hundreds, if not thousands, of processes. Mapping tools help us to visually see a process, analyze individual steps to determine their value, and identify improvement opportunities. The two most common mapping tools are process mapping (PM) and value-stream mapping (VSM). These two methods of visualizing a process are very different from basic flowcharts. Flowcharts provide a high level and simplified view of a process. Flowcharts are a communication tool, not a process improvement tool. PM and VSM are specifically designed for process improvement in that they consist of three major components:

1. Current state map – A map of the current process
2. Future state map – A map of the proposed new and improved process
3. Improvement plan – An action plan detailing the steps or tasks needed to achieve the future state with completion dates and staff assignments

Each of these tools can be used and adapted to all types of environments but they have their differences. Picking the correct tool for the job is just as important in Lean as it is for carpenters, mechanics, and plumbers. Most colleges/universities use one or the other of these mapping tools, but I have yet to see one use both. I am going to share with you the similarities and differences of these tools and explain why I prefer process mapping for reviewing college processes.

## 5.1.1 Process Mapping

Effective PM provides all the detailed steps of a process. Process maps are generally easy for people to grasp because they are developed using basic shapes, terminology, and an easy to read design. Remember the coffee example that was discussed in Chapter 3? This is a process map where we used boxes to document all the steps, both VA and NVA, involved in making coffee. It was easy to read and to follow.

To create an effective process map, however, it's important to map until you reach the level of detail where you can see problems exist. The most common error when learning to process map is not going deep enough into the details, or the "weeds" so to speak, to expose the problems. People who are new to process mapping generally capture the broader or major steps in the process and omit the smaller detailed steps that a new person learning the job would need to know. If we use our coffee example again, a person new or inexperienced with mapping would likely capture the broader VA steps (top boxes in Figure 5.1), such as locating the coffee pot, inserting the

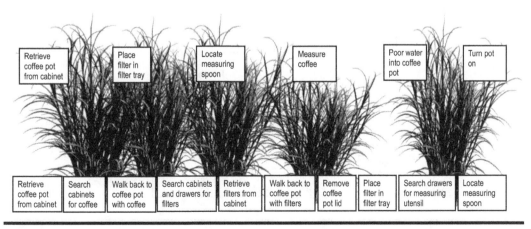

**Figure 5.1  Mapping Depth**

filter, and locating the measuring spoon. They would likely skip over many of the actual steps of searching, walking, locating, and repositioning items (lower boxes in Figure 5.1) which someone observing the task would see. If someone has been in a job for a while they may no longer be consciously aware of all the little (detailed) steps because they just do them without thinking. I often tell new mapping facilitators to "Take the role of a new employee learning the job. Ask for the detailed steps you would need to know to complete the task." It's important in PM to identify those detailed steps because that is often where the majority of the wastes are hidden.

Process maps are generally created by hanging long sections (approximately 10 feet) of butcher block paper on the wall. The most popular method of process mapping is to arrange the map into swim lanes (see Figure 5.2). The map is set up similar to lanes in a swimming pool. Each lane represents a person or department that has a responsibility in the process, often referred to as process stakeholders. Individual steps in the process are then written on sticky notes and placed in the appropriate swim lanes to map the process. Swim lanes make it easy to distinguish responsibility of tasks and show where handoffs (steps crossing into other swim lanes) are made to other departments or people. Handoffs are often where problems

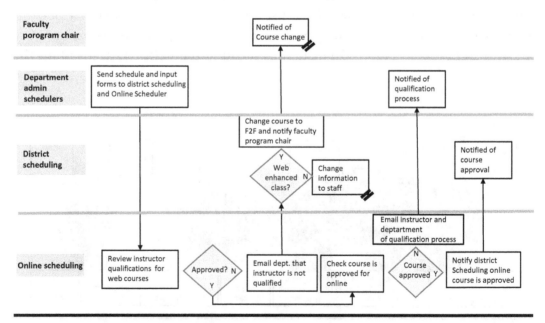

**Figure 5.2   Process Mapping with Swim Lanes**

and delays occur. The more handoffs and decisions you have in a process the slower your process usually is.

Decision points are another critical part of a process map. Decision points are represented by blue diamonds with a question written on them that can be answered with a *yes* (Y) or *no* (N). An example would be "Is the form complete?" A "Y" would be placed in one corner of the diamond and an "N" would be in a different corner. The group would then need to map the steps for both answers. Decision points show where and what type of decisions are being made in the process. Diving deeper into the reason for each decision often reveals that it is the result of earlier problems that were not corrected.

In addition to decisions, the number of steps, and handoffs, process maps can also reveal rework loops (where the process goes backwards), number of approvals/signatures, number of copies being made, number of tracking systems or spreadsheets involved, and more.

Process maps work best when working with processes where work is less repetitive (i.e. offices), less visual, and where it is important to understand the details, decisions, and types of handoffs being made, more than knowing the time it takes for each process step. You can, however, adapt it to include time, which is usually why some institutions choose to use VSM rather than PM – the main component of a value-stream map is conducting time studies.

Collecting cycle times is a good way to measure whether a process has improved and by how much. Cycle time is the time it takes for a worker to complete a task. For example, the time it takes for admissions to process an application or a supervisor to review an employee's timesheet. Gathering cycle times is a standard part of creating a value-stream map. Should you choose to, you can incorporate cycle time data into your process map in a couple of different ways. One way is to simply ask the workers who do the tasks on a regular basis how long it takes to do specific steps. They are usually pretty accurate.

In working with a large state university on their hiring process, we segmented the steps out and asked participants in the process what the high, average, and low times were for completing each segment. Then we added them all up to get a high, average, and low time for the entire process. This is called the process *lead time*, the time it takes to complete the process from the beginning to the end. Ironically, by the end of the training the HR director was able to pull data from their system which verified our numbers were accurate. Colette Williams,

Assistant Director University Process Improvement for the University of Memphis, has made capturing time a standard part of her PM events. Stakeholders within her project teams are asked to determine processing time for each swim lane. Times for each swim lane are then added together to get the total process or lead time. Her teams capture time for both the current process and the new implemented process as part of their standard metrics.

Another, more formal, way to capture time is to do actual time studies. For this you actually observe the person doing the task several times and time them with a stopwatch. This requires more time but allows for opportunities to also observe wastes occurring within each step.

Other benefits of process maps, due to their level of detail, is that they can be incorporated into training documents to help train new department employees. Table 5.1 provides examples of processes that I have mapped using process mapping and the type of organization it was for.

### 5.1.2 Value-Stream Mapping

Value-stream maps were designed initially in the manufacturing arena to help managers see major functions in a process, identify lead times for products and services, and identify where NVA activities existed.

Although VSM can be used to map detailed steps of a process, these maps generally display a process at a higher level showing the major functions (recruiting, admissions, registration), rather than individual process steps.

Since VSM is much more focused on time and product flow, mappers must conduct observations of the work being done and collect data that often includes the following:

■ cycle times for each function
■ inventory – Number of items waiting to be processed or the wait time between each function
■ quality levels – Percentage of items that have no errors
■ staffing numbers
■ customer demand – How many units must be produced or processed to meet customer demand in a given time period

Similar to how process maps are built, a long section of butcher block paper is posted on the wall. Participants begin building the map using sticky notes

**Table 5.1  Processes Evaluated – Examples**

| Process | Educ | Mfg | Serv | Govt | Process | Educ | Mfg | Serv | Govt |
|---|---|---|---|---|---|---|---|---|---|
| Accounts payable | X | X | X | X | Mowing services | | | | X |
| Accounts receivable | X | X | X | X | Multi-agency client services | X | | X | X |
| Admissions | X | | | | New student process admissions through registration | X | | | |
| Asset management | X | | | | Non-credit course scheduling | X | | | |
| Book advances for clock hour students | X | | | | Nuisance management | | | | X |
| Bookstore services | X | | | | Open class set-up | X | | | |
| Building permits | | | | X | Order processing | | X | | |
| Building/remodeling Requests | X | | | | Patents | | | X | |
| Career Advantage (High school dual enrollment) | X | | | | Payroll | X | | | X |
| Center for Working Families services integration | X | | | | PC lifecycle – request through retirement | | | X | |

(Continued)

**Table 5.1  (Cont.)**

| Process | Educ | Mfg | Serv | Govt |
|---|---|---|---|---|
| Citizen complaints | | | | X |
| Contracted training | X | | | |
| Counseling/advising | X | | | |
| Course assessment | X | | | |
| Course catalog production | X | | | |
| Course evaluations | X | | | |
| Credit for prior learning (grant) | X | | | |
| Curriculum commission/curriculum approval | X | | | |
| Customer services | X | | | X |
| Distance learning (online) course scheduling | X | | | |
| Employee complaints | | | | X |
| Employee off-boarding | X | | | |
| Employee on-boarding | X | | X | |
| ESL registration | X | | | |

| Process | Educ | Mfg | Serv | Govt |
|---|---|---|---|---|
| Pool maintenance | | | | X |
| Printing | | | X | |
| Procurement/purchasing | X | | X | X |
| Product processing | | X | X | |
| Program concentrations (in SIS) | X | | | |
| Program waitlist | X | | | |
| Recruitment | X | | X | |
| Registration (student) | X | | | |
| Remodel requests | X | | | |
| Sales orders | | X | | |
| Scheduling | X | | X | |
| Scholarship application and awarding | X | | | |
| Six Sigma Green Belt training process | | | X | |
| Special events planning | | | | X |

| Process | | | |
|---|---|---|---|
| Financial aid | X | | |
| Foundation (scholarships, events) | X | | |
| Graduation | X | | |
| Grant programs (service, delivery and management) | X | X | |
| High school completion | X | | |
| Hiring (FT, PT, student, adjunct) | X | X | |
| Hiring (parks/pool staff) | | X | |
| Home inspections | | X | X |
| HVAC material procurement and service | X | | |
| Incident investigation | X | | |
| Insurance processing | X | | |
| Insurance re-rates | X | | |
| Integrated services (multi-agency) | X | | |

| Process | | | |
|---|---|---|---|
| Student accounts | X | | |
| Student orientation | X | | |
| Student onboarding | X | | |
| Student verification of enrollment | X | | |
| Testing (education) | X | | |
| Trademark application | | X | |
| Transcript processing | X | | |
| Vehicle maintenance scheduling | | | X |
| Warehousing | | X | |
| Water and environmental Programs Applications | | | X |
| Water/gas disconnect and reconnect | | | X |
| Water/soil testing | | X | |
| Workforce training program | X | X | |

(Continued)

**Table 5.1 (Cont.)**

| Process | Educ | Mfg | Serv | Govt | Process | Educ | Mfg | Serv | Govt |
|---|---|---|---|---|---|---|---|---|---|
| International admissions | X | | | | | | | | |
| Leave requests | X | | | | | | | | |
| Marketing material production | | | X | | | | | | |
| membership services | | | | X | | | | | |
| | | | | | | | | | |

Edu – education (higher education and K12)
Mfg – manufacturing
Serv – service (insurance, call centers, consumer, non-profit, for profit)
Govt – government (state and local)

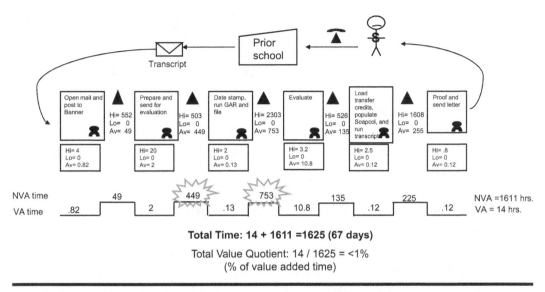

**Figure 5.3    Value-Stream Map: Reverse Transcript Process**

and data that was collected during their observations. Swim lanes are not used in this type of mapping. Generally the map is divided into a top and bottom section (see Figure 5.3). The top half of the paper shows information flow while the bottom shows product flow. However, some users have modified it so that both information and product are mapped together in one line.

Once the steps are mapped, data boxes are added under the steps to display cycle times, quality, and other relevant information. Cycle times represent the VA part of the process. Between each step, a triangle icon is drawn and the inventory/wait time data is added beneath it. These represent the NVA parts of the process.

At the very bottom of the map a *lead time ladder* is drawn. Both VA and NVA times are brought down and added to the ladder using similar units of measurement (i.e. minutes, seconds, hours, days).

Finally, all the VA times are added up to determine the *processing time* which is the amount of time the product is actually being worked on. This does not include the amount of time it spends just waiting or traveling about. All the NVA times are also added up to determine the production *lead time*. Lead time is the amount of time it takes to make it through the process from beginning to end. This is always much longer than the processing time. In the reverse transcript process (Figure 5.3) the transcript took on average 14 hours (*processing time*) but it was in the system for 1611 hours (lead time).

Most of that time it was just waiting for the next step to occur or it was in transit to another office, both NVA activities. It is not uncommon to see processes with less than 5% VA time, especially if Lean is not practiced.

Information shown on value-stream maps is intended to identify where process flow is being impeded and where waste exists so improvements can be made. Over the years many organizations and colleges/universities have adapted VSM for office processes. I started out using VSM in manufacturing. It was the only form of mapping I used for several years. When I started doing more work in office type settings, VSM just didn't seem to fit as well. I've been using both types of mapping tools for years. I've even merged elements of the two mapping tools together based on the needs of the customer.

Even though I used VSM regularly and saw its benefits, I also saw problems with it. One concern I had was that it is not intuitive enough for people to continue using long term unless they are a practitioner regularly leading events. Value-stream maps involve significant amounts of data collection and data calculations which add to its difficulty level. Most participants need close guidance to know what data to collect and how to then calculate lead times and processing times. There are also a significant number of different icons and terms for people to remember and know how to use. Process maps average around five icons whereas value-stream maps average more than twelve. In addition, terms such as cycle time, process time, takt time, Kanban, kaizen burst, push, pull, lead time, and demand rate are generally foreign to people who do not work in manufacturing.

Coming from a background of teaching middle school I like to keep things simple. If it's simple people are more likely to understand it and use it. Most people unfamiliar with PM can read and understand a process map. People unfamiliar with VSM cannot read a value-stream map without some type of introduction or training.

My final concern is that because value-stream maps are usually mapped at a higher level with less detail they often don't dive deep enough into the details to expose the root cause of problems. Cycle times may show where a problem lies but not enough specific details about the problem to allow you to solve it. It is placed on an action register for further evaluation and review (aka another committee or meeting). In contrast, a significantly higher number of solutions are identified during a PM event due to the level of detail that is being reviewed.

As I mentioned earlier, some institutions have found ways to adapt VSM to meet their needs. It is a useful tool that has a place and a purpose but

| Process Map | Value-Stream Map |
|---|---|
| • Level of difficulty = low to medium | • Level of difficulty = medium to high |
| • Provides a detailed view of a process | • Shows major functions within a process (recruitment, admissions, advising, registration) |
| • Shows specific tasks within a function | • Shows cycle times for each function-how long it takes to do that function |
| • Shows decision points | |
| • Shows where the process crosses departments or functions (handoffs) | • Shows inventory and/or wait time between the functions |
| • Shows specific locations of all opportunities and generates detailed ideas for improvement | • Shows overall value-added and non-value-added time within a process |
| • Can be used as a training document | • Shows where the greatest opportunities for improvement exist |
| **Use when:** | **Use when:** |
| • working with specific departments or work groups on a single process | • working with senior management to make strategic decisions |
| • standard work does not exist | • a 'big picture' view is needed (door-to-door) |
| • working with front-line workers to solve daily problems | • working with major functions or departments |
| • you want to see where specific handoffs between departments occur | • you want to distinguish between information flow and product flow |
| • you want to determine what decisions are made in the process and when | • lead times, cycle times, inventory levels and various process metrics are important |
| • working with areas that have high variability in job tasks | • working with production areas characterized by having inventory, repetitive work, machinery, and product flow |

**Figure 5.4   Mapping Tools: Which to Use**

I believe PM is a better, simpler tool for someone to use to begin a Lean journey. People who participate in a process mapping session are typically able to pick up the mechanics of it quickly and at times help create the map. I've even observed past process map participants create their own mini-process maps in later meetings as they try to figure out a new or troublesome process. Not once have I observed a person working on an individual value-stream map in a meeting as they try to figure out process problems. Today if I'm in an office or transactional environment I will use PM unless the needs of the customer align more with what VSM provides (see Figure 5.4). By the same token, if I'm in a manufacturing or production environment I will use VSM unless the needs of the customer align better with PM.

## 5.2  5S: Organizing Workspaces Tool

Another tool that I would recommend for anyone starting on their Lean journey is 5S. Originating with Toyota, 5S is a structured approach to organizing workspaces to improve efficiency and effectiveness. It consists of 5 steps, each starting with the letter S (sort, set in order, shine, standardize, and sustain), thus 5S. Since it was designed by a Japanese company you will often see the untranslated steps listed as seiri, seiton, seiso, seiketsu, and shitsuke. You may not have heard of 5S, but today the internet is filled with examples of "life hacks" which are basically simple innovative ways to make things simple and efficient, which is the basis of 5S.

Most of us keep way more "stuff" than we need to do our jobs. Remember the waste of *excess inventory* and *excess motion* discussed in Chapter 4? The 5S tool works directly to minimize and eliminate those two wastes. It's a tool that can be used with individuals, groups, faculty, staff, students, and entire departments. People who learn how to use the tool often end up using it at home. It is a powerful tool because it provides immediate results and gives back a sense of control to those who implement it.

I want to share with you a few examples of how 5S can benefit individuals. One of my favorite examples is of a woman who worked on one of our satellite campuses. I will call her Sheila. She was a financial aid specialist responsible for assisting students with their financial aid applications. Sheila's office was disorganized, with at least 20 binders lining her work surfaces, tops of cabinets, and overhead storage units. Her work surfaces were cluttered with papers, folders, personal items, and mail that had flooded over onto the floor where it mixed with boxes, promotional water bottles, various bags, beverage cans, reams of paper, posters, and other clutter. For added work space she had an adjustable drafting table positioned next to her desk where students would sit and fill out paperwork. The space fell far below expectations for impressing potential students and parents.

To Sheila's credit, she was very student focused. She was like many people I have encountered over the years in that she was aware of her problem but had no idea how to go about fixing it. Many people in this type of situation see the task as overwhelming and become paralyzed. Seeing an opportunity, I would stop in for a quick chat whenever I was on campus hoping to build trust and hopefully persuade her to allow me to help. During those short conversations I quickly realized that Sheila was in fact embarrassed by her disorganization and deep down desired something better. She eventually agreed to let me work with her a couple times a week for a few hours, which also made her provost very happy. I started by asking her what she envisioned for her space and she replied, "I always wanted an office with nice pictures on the wall."

I smiled at the simplicity of her goal and promised we could make that happen and a lot more. Then, we set to work on the 5-step program to organize her workspace.

1. Sort – Sort is the first step. In this step you literally sort through everything, identify what's needed, what is not, and remove anything that is not needed. During this step you also look at the items you need and determine the appropriate quantity to keep on hand. This requires going through every drawer, folder, bookcase, organizer, storage cabinet, shelf, and work surface to determine each item's value and needed quantity. Yes, this is time consuming, especially if you do not have a regular practice of sorting out unneeded items.

In Sheila's office we went through *everything*! We were able to eliminate almost all of her binders which contained outdated, unneeded, and duplicate information. In some of them she had several years of financial aid documents that she thought she needed to keep. I requested she call the financial aid director on the main campus and ask about retention of the documents. I already knew the answer she would get but needed her to hear it first-hand. She learned that the main financial aid office was the official custodian and therefore her unofficial copies could be shredded. Not quite trusting that it was okay to shred her copies, she decided to hang onto a year's worth of documents. To help her see that she really didn't need them, I asked her to store them in a place outside her office. Then, if she really needed them she would have to make an extra effort to retrieve them. We chose a storage room down the hall. Doing this made her more aware of how often she accessed the copies. Less than four months later I saw her at a campus event where she proudly announced that she had shredded all the past documents, keeping only the documents for the current semester. Sheila ended up eliminating excess filing cabinets, reference materials, office supplies, and personal items freeing up significant space in her office.

2. Set in order – This step follows sort and its purpose is to have you evaluate your remaining needed items and arrange them in the most efficient location based on your workflow, frequency of use, and the quantity needed. Items used regularly should be located closest to you. The less you use something the farther away it should be stored. Every

item should have a designated storage space and be in its space. Spaces should be limited to hold only what is needed for a reasonable period of time (i.e. a week or month). An example would be to create a space only big enough to store one ream of paper vs. an entire box that would last 6 months.

'Set in order' for Sheila involved organizing her office layout so she had everything she needed to work with students in one place. In addition, we determined it would be more efficient to create an Excel spreadsheet with all her Banner (student information system) codes rather than storing paper copies in various binders. We placed a shortcut (link) to the excel document on her computer desktop so she could access it easily and I showed her how to quickly create, update, and search for codes in seconds vs. the time she was spending printing, sorting, and searching with her previous binder system. We also eliminated her drafting table, two filing cabinets, and replaced her old inadequate office furniture with a repurposed office unit from a remodel on another campus.

3. Shine – This step is usually done at the same time as the set in order step. The purpose of this step is to clean everything inside and out and to inspect items and equipment while you are cleaning them. This is to ensure they are in good working order, to make your space easy to clean, and ensure proper cleaning supplies are easily accessible for future cleaning.

Now that Sheila had a desk with overhead storage and she was able to eliminate stacks of unneeded items, she made it a personal rule to store nothing on the floor. People by nature do not move things on the floor to clean. They clean around them causing them to become even more dirty and cluttered. Sheila re-located her trash and recycle bins for easier access, installed simple organizers to store paperwork and supplies, and stocked a few cleaning supplies in her overhead storage for easy access.

4. Standardize – Once you have things in their proper location the idea is to make visual indicators so everyone knows where items belong. The purpose of this step is to make standard conditions obvious by creating simple visual controls. Visuals consist of lines, signs, labels, color-coding, symbols, and instructions. Think about driving through the city and all the visual controls that help you and everyone else navigate

properly and avoid accidents. Even parking in a parking lot we have visual controls (painted lines) that tell us where to park. Now, imagine if those visuals were not there. How would your experience change? How much more chaotic, inefficient, and hazardous would your experience be? Visuals should make it obvious and easy for people to do the right thing and to help ensure the level of organization in the workspace is maintained. This step often includes training as well to properly explain the new standards and expectations for the area.

In Sheila's office we organized folders and files by categories of work and color-coded them for easy identification. Standard naming conventions were established for both her physical and electronic files to save time searching and to eliminate redundancy. We created reorder/replenishment cards to trigger timely restocking of essential supplies such as forms, brochures, and information packets. In addition, we labeled all her designated storage locations and frequent work items throughout her office. We also designed visual instructions for students to help with tasks and created visual aids for infrequent office procedures.

5. Sustain – This is the last and most difficult step in the process. The goal of this step is to create a plan to keep the workspace organized going forward and to create daily organizing habits. For offices it involves setting document retention limits, scheduling regular times to perform daily, monthly and yearly 5S activities and creating a process to ensure everyone is working to sustain the improvements.

My hat goes off to Sheila as she was able to keep her office clean and organized for the next several years until she retired. I did a quick check whenever I was on campus and always commented how well she was doing. She achieved the goal of having nice pictures on the wall in addition to working more efficiently, having pride in her space, and learning skills that she ended up using at home.

5S is a tool that can provide immediate results for people across the educational institution. When I am out working with colleges/universities I frequently get asked, "How do you get faculty more involved." 5S is one way. I've worked with healthcare faculty on five campuses to organize storerooms, classrooms, and labs. I've assisted culinary arts faculty to organize kitchens and storerooms and trained automotive faculty to organize offices, classrooms, and shop areas. I've also assisted exercise science faculty to organize exercise spaces, offices, and storerooms. In has also been particularly satisfying to help individuals from across the institution apply 5S to physical and electronic space to improve their daily work. It's a great tool that can help people work smarter and not harder every day.

There are many other Lean tools available, but limiting it to just a select few in the beginning helps launch your program more quickly and reduce the initial learning curve for both new facilitators and participants.

# Chapter 6

# Do Your Research

Although Lean has been around for decades, if you've done any research prior to this book, you've likely discovered that there are not a lot of guide books or resources available to assist higher education institutions in getting started with Lean. Much of what has been written focuses on manufacturing which has been practicing Lean since the days of Henry Ford. What has been done in higher education up until now is a combination of trying to adapt manufacturing methods to fit higher education settings and lots of trial and error. I'm also here to tell you that there is no magic bullet, instruction guide, or single method for an improvement approach. It's a wide topic that can quickly overwhelm anyone that's new to it.

Thus far in this book you have learned about what Lean/continuous improvement is, about wastes, and about Lean tools. If you are interested in developing a Lean program for your educational institution, the remainder of this book will serve as a guide to building your program.

As you learn more about Lean and do more with it, your job will be to find, develop, and adapt methods that work best for your institution. This recommendation includes the information provided in this book. If it doesn't feel right or work right, change it, adapt it, and make it fit your environment.

Begin by building your knowledge around Lean, continuous improvement, and process improvement. This can be done in a variety of ways and should include finding others who are already doing formalized continuous improvement. Look at what they are doing and how they are doing it. Look for common themes, methods, best practices, and ask for advice. Search the internet and inquire with other colleges and networking groups. Research information on institutions similar to your own and also some that are different. A good research resource within higher education is LeanHE[1] which is a peer organization for people working to apply Lean and similar approaches in higher education.

A good starting point is to research other organizations doing Lean including healthcare, manufacturing, government, and service providers. Even though you are not a manufacturing business, there is still knowledge to be gained from hearing and seeing Lean concepts and tools in practice from someone who has been doing it for years. An additional benefit is that manufacturing is visual. In that environment you can see process flow in action. However, much of what we do in education is invisible, meaning it is information that moves around on paper, through systems, and in the cloud. It's hard to see how a process flows unless you physically map it by identifying each step on paper (see Chapter 5, heading 5.1 Mapping Tools).

Things to look for and take note of in your research with others doing Lean/continuous improvement include the following:

■ Internal support structure – Who leads the continuous improvement charge? Is there a staff dedicated to continuous improvement? What responsibility does each level of the organization have in supporting Lean activities? How do they ensure everyone is involved? How is it promoted internally? How are projects/activities identified and selected? How do they keep it going? Are improvements shared across the institution/organization?

■ Methods, tools, and models used – How are employees educated about Lean? Is it through on-going training, department meetings, department activities, or solely by participation on projects? What tools are used to evaluate processes, organize workspaces and solve problems? Look for examples of tools being utilized such as PM, VSM, 5S, A3, kaizen, Six Sigma, etc. Are their methods of delivering the Lean tools standardized or do they vary each time? For example, if they map a process do they follow the same steps to set it up, train, identify improvements, and monitor implementation? Does the process have a repeatable cycle?

■ Performance metrics – Are metrics collected? If so, what's the expectation? For example, are there goals on cost savings/cost avoidance? Are those goals expected to align with strategic initiatives or show a return on investment?

- Case studies – Do they have specific examples of projects, successes, and challenges from their institution? Would they be willing to share those with you?
- Resources – Do they utilize internal staff, external consultants, or a combination to facilitate, train or support lean activities? Is there a steering team to help guide the direction of Lean activities? Do they have training curriculum (presentation slides, trainer guides, participant manuals)?
- Funding – Have they allocated funds to help support and implement changes?

Other ideas for building your knowledge of Lean:

- Utilize your Lean connections. Don't be afraid to ask if you can sit in and observe a process improvement event at companies or educational institutions doing continuous improvement. They may be open to it and what you observe and learn may spark ideas for your own program.
- Sign up for Lean classes. Lean focuses on tools that help remove wastes in processes. There may be Lean consulting groups or community colleges/universities offering classes in your area. I recommend starting with an introductory Lean class that provides an overview of Lean and common tools. Then deepen your knowledge of Lean with classes on specific tools such as 5S, process mapping, value stream mapping, standard work, and A3.
I would recommend *not* using Six Sigma classes as your starting point for learning about Lean/continuous improvement. Six Sigma is a good method but is best kept for later use. Six Sigma focuses on reducing and controlling process variability. It relies heavily on statistical analysis and has a much steeper learning curve than other methods. Consensus among many continuous improvement practitioners is to start with Lean to clean up the processes and then utilize Six Sigma later on to refine the processes. Several companies I've worked with in the past who did start with Six Sigma are now advising others to begin with Lean first. In addition, it is likely that only continuous improvement staff would be the ones to use and lead Six Sigma methods due to its complexity.
I once had a company use Lean to review their Six Sigma Green Belt certification process. Ironically, they were training large numbers of employees in Six Sigma but very few ever finished their certification. In other words, they didn't complete their projects.

I also had an HR department that was resistant to learning a new process improvement tool because of their previous experience with Six Sigma projects. After some convincing they agreed to a PM event and loved how simple it was. Again, Six Sigma is a good tool, just not the best one to introduce and initiate a Lean/continuous improvement program.

■ Consider hiring experienced Lean trainers to teach courses on Lean methods and tools at your institution. Most of the community colleges in the state of Iowa and other states in the US offer non-credit Lean classes through their continuing education departments, or other departments that work closely with business and industry. The classes generate revenue but can also help off-set the cost of training for internal staff. It's also a way to connect with trainers and outside organizations that may already be doing formal continuous improvement.

■ Hire experienced trainers to conduct classes on various tools and/or to lead projects within your institution. This allows you and other college/university stakeholders to test Lean methods, get an idea of potential benefits, and gauge receptivity within your institution and with employees.

In summary, doing your research will save you a great deal of time and frustration moving forward with initiating Lean at your institution. You are not likely to find a canned (one-size-fits-all) Lean product that will easily fit your institution's needs and culture. However, you will identify components, best practices and advice to help build your own model and approach.

## Note

1 www.leanhe.org/lean-he.

# Chapter 7

## Determine Budget and Who's Driving Your Efforts

### 7.1 Budgeting

Anything worth doing is worth doing right. Anything worth doing right usually requires funding. Through your research you've hopefully begun gathering estimated costs and outlining a preliminary plan for what you'd like to do at your institution. If not, reconnect with those institutions with programs already in place to ask if they'd be willing to share budget information to help with your planning. Here are some basic costs to consider when building your budget:

- External consultant fees (facilitation, travel, materials, curriculum development) – estimate the number of training/consulting events you are planning for in the first year or needed to get you started. Determine the rates for each type of activity. Consider whether the consultants/trainers are local or coming from far away. Are materials included with the trainings or in addition to? Do they charge for developing/customizing the trainings or do they already have programs available?
- Internal Lean facilitator(s)
  - Salary, benefits
  - Office/technology – Office space, computers, projectors, phones, furniture
  - Travel – Between locations and for professional development

- Professional development – Number and type of programs/events, locations, costs
- Training materials and supplies – Books, curriculum, supplies, printing

■ Lean event/training costs – Food, refreshments, room rental, travel (if participating employees are traveling between sites)

■ Implementation/innovation fund – Lean project teams will identify many improvement ideas. Some will only cost staff time but others will require funding for technology programming, equipment, software, specialized training, additional staffing, etc. An implementation/innovation fund would provide pre-allocated funding for one-time investments leading to long term efficiencies, improvements, and growth. Ideally, you want the realized cost savings redeposited back into the fund to make it self-sustaining for future innovations.

Once you've managed to gather and outline a preliminary budget, leaders need to decide whether the institution is willing to invest dollars and staff time to fuel this initiative. If the answer is "no" or "not yet" your journey likely ends here or you can achieve some success applying process improvement within individual departments. Unfortunately the benefits often stop once processes cross into departments where continuous improvement is not practiced or supported. If the answer to the investment question is "yes" then the journey continues which leads us to hiring a facilitator.

## 7.2 Hiring the Facilitator

Obviously, one of the biggest budget items you will initially face is determining who will drive your continuous improvement efforts. Who will lead the day-to-day efforts? Whether you are utilizing an external consultant, hiring a new staff position, reassigning internal staff, or assigning the duties to a chosen employee, it's important to select the right person with the correct skills and personality for the job. Hire the wrong person and the whole thing falls apart. Too often I've witnessed organizations simply assign process improvement duties to someone's existing workload, usually with little consideration given to the person's level of interest, knowledge, or skill level regarding Lean. From my previous work and observations I would suggest you *do not* hire or assign a Lean facilitator who is not passionate about working with people, process improvement, or problem-solving. It is critical that the person or persons have strong facilitation skills. Facilitation is different from presentation and teaching skills. In both teaching and presentations you usually have prepared materials and the information being delivered has a prescribed beginning, middle, and end point. Facilitation, however, requires that the person also be able to adapt to all types of situations and personalities. They need to be able to constantly re-assess and adjust to the needs of the group and changing information. They need to listen well and manage the environment in order to guide the group to a resolution or plan of action within the prescribed timeframe.

A good facilitator must be:

- Flexible and adaptable – Able to react to and manage changes in information, personalities, group dynamics, and situations
- Able to multi-task – Listen, process information, visualize next steps, and manage group dynamics all at the same time
- Have strong relationship skills – Be personable, respectful, and approachable
- Have excellent problem-solving skills – Know what questions to ask and have experience with utilizing problem solving tools to identify root causes and develop improvement solutions
- Capable of reading an audience and drawing out critical information through questioning, use of tools/methods, and personal interactions
- Organized – Be prepared and able to manage training logistics, content, supplies, communications, and project documentation

Choosing the right person to lead your Lean activities is just as important as hiring a qualified person to lead any department. Think seriously about what is needed to move your process improvement activities forward and what your budget will allow. Below are options for securing a facilitator.

## 7.2.1 External Consultant/Trainers

If you do not have internal staff with adequate time and skills to lead your initial Lean activities consider hiring an external consultant/trainer. You can choose to hire them on a long term contract to lead your activities for months or years, or on a shorter term basis to get you started. Institutions often use external consultants/trainers to conduct pilot projects, train internal facilitators, or fill the gap until a full-time facilitator can be on-boarded.

When hiring an external consultant/trainer make sure the person has a solid background in continuous improvement *and* has proven experience working with colleges/universities. There have been many instances of colleges hiring process improvement experts from manufacturing to lead activities in higher education. Although a few have been successful, many participants have been left with negative feelings about the experience. Having worked and led process improvement for many years in both manufacturing and higher education, I will tell you they are *NOT* the same. The tools and methods may be similar but the focus, design, culture, and terminology are different.[1] Continuous process improvement is hard enough. Why make it harder by trying to fit a square peg (manufacturing methods) into a round hole (educational needs)?

Once you have identified the right external person for the job, contact them immediately to begin devising a plan and scope of service. For example, will they lead specific training events to get you started, train other facilitators, or act as a fulltime staff member for an extended time period to establish your program? Determine if they already have a training curriculum or if they will develop a program just for you. If they have already developed and are using their own training materials, check to see if there is an option to purchase the materials for long term use such as trainer guides, PowerPoint presentations, participant manuals, and templates. If they are not an employee of your institution (remain an independent consultant) and they do not plan to charge you for development of the materials, they retain curriculum rights unless you make arrangements to purchase the materials. If you are paying for them to develop a curriculum make sure you specify your rights to that curriculum after you discontinue using them as a facilitator. This is important because it can cause problems if you stop using that consultant/trainer and a prior arrangement for the materials has not been agreed to in writing.

## 7.2.2 Internal Staff

If your plan is to have an employee within your institution coordinate and deliver your Lean activities consider these options.

1. Hire a new employee who is experienced in process improvement. Finding someone with experience can be difficult and expensive. There are not a lot of educational or training programs available to adequately prepare someone in process improvement. Almost all of the experienced

practitioners I know gained their knowledge on the job and by attending Lean classes when available.

2. Reassign one or more existing employees who already have some Lean/ process improvement skills. This will likely be more cost-effective than Option 1 but it may take longer to launch your efforts depending on experience level.

3. Reassign an existing employee with intuitive problem-solving skills and train them in formal process improvement tools. This is a much slower process due to the fact that it will take time to get the person up to speed. It's difficult to find good quality training programs and materials to adequately prepare someone with little to no prior background in continuous improvement. However, if you already have an experienced person (internal or external) leading activities, this option can be used to develop additional inexperienced trainers.

Next, determine whether the position will be fully or partially dedicated to continuous improvement activities. If it is not a fully dedicated position be cautious. If the position is partially dedicated and the Lean portion of the job is not given at least equal priority to that person's other responsibilities, it could lead to problems. Lower priority equates to less time which may lead to your Lean initiative quickly running out of steam. By the same measure, if the person is not passionate about continuous improvement they will naturally give it lower priority.

Once you've determined how you will fill the position the best practice is to have the position report to a senior leader such as office of the president, CFO, vice-presidents, or some other higher level position. This allows the facilitator to hold an impartial view of the institution because they are not aligned with any particular department. It also provides a level of perceived power when dealing with resistors and helps ensure their activities align with broader institutional goals.

## 7.2.3 Combination of Resources

Depending on who's available and your budget, you may need to use a combination of various consultants and facilitators based on the different skill sets needed. One possibility is to use external trainers and consultants to train the masses or fill the training gaps that your internal continuous improvement staff can't provide. In another scenario, maybe someone, an external consultant, is good at leadership development and strategy deployment, another at process mapping, and possibly your internal person is good at meeting facilitation. You are the client so get the different entities to work together to build a training program that works for you.

With regard to Lean staffing, I recommend at some point having internal, dedicated, continuous improvement staff if you are serious about Lean and changing your culture. A review of colleges/universities around the world who have established continuous improvement programs found many to employ one to three dedicated staff members who lead improvement activities and train employees. The University of Memphis in Tennessee hired an internal continuous improvement staff person and utilized an external consulting firm to provide initial training (Williams and Stewart, 2019). Ivy Tech Community College in Indiana hired two internal staff for their initiative and used an outside consultant to provide some initial training (Moreland, 2018). The University of Sheffield in England also hired two internal staff members after their attempt to find an external hire with the desired qualifications was unsuccessful (McAssey, 2019).[2]

Once you have decided on whether to utilize an external Lean/continuous improvement consultant or create an internal position, the next step would be for the appropriate budget manager and HR staff to determine how to fill the position and secure the resources for that position.

## 7.3 Lean Advisory (Steering) Committee

In addition to someone to lead your events, at some point I encourage you to consider forming an advisory committee to help drive continuous improvement throughout your institution. Seventy percent of the institutions that I interviewed for this book have formal advisory/steering committees of some sort that oversee their continuous improvement activities. Some did not initially start out with an advisory committee but later added one to sustain their continuous improvement momentum.

If you choose to create an advisory committee early in your journey this group would be tasked with most of the decision making and planning for getting your Lean program off the ground including hiring a facilitator. For these reasons there would need to be higher level leaders with approval authority involved. Depending on your institution, your initial committee may be part of an existing cross-functional group or it could be a completely new one. Once your program is up and running you may decide to change the make-up of the group to one with a balance of leadership, staff, faculty, and representative of areas across the institution.

Advisory committees are generally tasked with ensuring that Lean efforts align with institutional goals. Other duties often include helping to plan and drive improvement activities, monitoring outcomes, communicating results, and helping to evaluate and improve the overall Lean program. They can be effective in identifying gaps and addressing barriers to progress. Ultimately, the goal is to achieve a true Lean culture where everyone in the organization is using and actively promoting process improvement behaviors. The more people there are to help internally drive and market your continuous improvement program the better.

## Notes

1  Manufacturing focuses more on inventory, throughput, changeover time, cost, and scrap while education focuses more on decisions, hand-offs, access to information, and delivery of service.
2  The number of dedicated continuous improvement staff by college: Des Moines Area Community College (2), University of Sheffield (2.5), University of Memphis (3), Everett Community College (1), Blue Community College (1), Berea College (2).

## References

McAssey, R. 2019. Lean Program Questions [Email].
Moreland, K. 2018. Lean in Higher Ed [Email].
Williams, C. and Stewart, R. 2019. Process Improvement Program Questions [Email].

## Chapter 8

# Determining Purpose

Once you've taken steps to onboard someone to lead/facilitate your activities, it's time to start building a plan to launch your continuous improvement program. The reason I placed this section after the chapter 'Determine Budget and Who's Driving Your Efforts' is because I believe the person who will be leading the efforts at your institution needs to be an integral part of creating the plan for continuous improvement at your institution.

As you begin taking steps to build your plan it's important to gain a firm understanding of why your institution is choosing to go down this continuous improvement path. Someone thought it was a good idea, so now it's time to put that thought into action. A good place to start is assembling key institutional leaders and staff who will be making your initial continuous improvement decisions for the institution. This group will be tasked with everything from identifying the purpose of your initiative through the scheduling of your first year's activities. As we discussed earlier, this could be your advisory committee or whatever group you have chosen to take on these responsibilities. Whomever you choose, try to keep the group size manageable but yet representative of the institution. To eliminate confusion, from this point forward I will refer to this group as your advisory committee.

Begin by scheduling committee work sessions. You and your facilitator can choose to schedule full day, half day, or shorter sessions to lay the groundwork for your program. I typically schedule full or half day sessions initially to work through items in this and the next chapter more quickly. These can range from several 2-hour sessions to full day workshops, depending on what works best for your institution. As part of the initial work session, have your Lean facilitator or consultant lead the committee through a basic overview of Lean: what it is, what it is not, and how Lean can help the institution in creating positive change. During the overview, drill deep (giving specific examples) into the different types of work wastes and how they impact daily performance. Give them a chance to discuss where they see waste existing and the problems they are causing for employees, students, and the institution. This is your first attempt to get the committee to start *seeing* waste. Document their wastes so they are visible and available for later use.

In addition to the wastes, provide an overview of some common Lean tools (Chapter 5) and methods, especially those that you hope to use from your research discussed in Chapter 6. I would also recommend a review of basic change-management principles for this committee since they are tasked with creating change. The assessment, the Lean overview, and the change-management component are all intended to begin exposing the issues/ opportunities that the Lean program is intended to help address.

Once the initial *training* is complete it's time to start working on building your program. The committee will be asked to work through the five questions that follow. I like to post flipcharts of each of these questions around the room and have the participants use brainstorming to answer each of them. Once all the questions have been answered, have the committee prioritize their answers for each question.

## 8.1 Why Lean and Why Now?

Your Lean advisory committee will start by determining the institutional "why." Why is the institution deciding to go down this Lean/continuous improvement path rather than remain as is? As you build your plan for launching Lean it will be important to communicate the reasons behind your decisions and also get everyone moving in the same direction. If you have not read John Kotter and Holger Rathgeber's book, *Our Iceberg is Melting* (2006) that might be a good book to read now. It's all about finding your sense of urgency, that urgent need to change in order to avoid impending negative effects looming on the horizon. That may sound dark and scary, right? Well, it can be if your institution isn't already looking ahead and finding ways to adapt.

What is the current state or condition of your institution? What challenges or critical situations are you facing? Is it budget? Is your enrollment growing or declining? Maybe it's lagging technology, or something else? What does the future look like for your institution? Are there other larger strategic issues at play? Have each member of the committee complete the Assessment of Institutional Challenges/Problems from Chapter 2 (Table 2.1). The purpose is to get them thinking about current institutional strengths and weaknesses that may affect long term institutional goals. Have them tally their responses and tabulate the results of the entire group. This should give you an indication of your institution's need for a continuous improvement program. Whether you have any of these concerns on the horizon or you are aspiring to be a flagship institution, this type of information will be important for communicating the need for change throughout the organization. If you have no urgent need it will be more difficult to get employees to initially buy-in and make change happen.

Des Moines Area Community College's sense of urgency was due to several factors. Student enrollment had grown 43% in 5 years, the state of Iowa drastically cut college funding, a large number of experienced employees were at retirement age, student and technology needs were rapidly changing, and they were preparing for an upcoming accreditation renewal.

Ivy Tech Community College, which serves the entire state of Indiana, needed to leverage economies of scale and was finding it difficult to provide cost-effective technology solutions when campuses and sites operated differently from one another.

Other colleges like West Shore Community College in Michigan and University of Sheffield in South Yorkshire, England had senior leaders who had the desire to do continuous improvement after seeing others use it successfully.

## 8.2 What Do You Expect to Achieve?

In addition to identifying your why or sense of urgency, the committee should next identify strategic goals or outcomes for which they are striving. Where are you headed as an institution? What are the plans for staying competitive, reducing costs, increasing services and how does Lean fit into all of these? What does success look like? Possible success goals might be to improve student access to quality services, reduce costs, to have all departments active in continuous improvement, to create a standard process for evaluating and prioritizing college improvements, and to create consistency across the institution. Get the committee to state what specifically they want to achieve with this initiative.

## 8.3 What Are the Benefits to the Organization?

Your benefits can mirror what you identified above but will hopefully narrow in on what the values are to your customers and students. Examples: reduce the need for (or amount of) tuition increase, reduce costs, improve service, increase retention, expand technology, reduce workload, upgrade technology, and become proactive vs. reactive in meeting customer/student needs. Basically, how will it impact your institution?

## 8.4 How Will It Benefit Employees?

Employees need to know how this initiative will impact them, their WIIFM (what's in it for me?). What can they expect and why should they care? Have the committee list the potential benefits they see for employees. Examples of common benefits to employees include: reduced frustration, minimization or elimination of errors, time saving, elimination of unnecessary steps, better understanding of work processes, respect for co-workers, and improved communications between and within departments. Lean also creates opportunities for employees to be a part of the change process. If they help to develop change for their department they will own it and are more likely to buy into it, implement it, and keep it moving. Engaged employees are more productive and you will likely find hidden talents that were previously under-utilized (remember the waste of under-utilized people).

## 8.5 Potential Impact of Inaction?

Sometimes the best way to convince the masses of what needs to be done is by providing perspective. It will be important to develop an awareness of how things are changing in higher education (Chapter 1) and the impact these changes are having on educational institutions. Then communicate the benefits of taking a proactive approach to the issues, as well as the impact of inaction. What effect will inaction have on student enrollment, accreditation, funding, services, and employee benefits? Draw from your research and assessment results (Chapter 2) and discuss national trends. ICEF Monitor (2018) reports that

■ The number of small US colleges forced to close each year has continued to climb from 2015 levels
■ The growing number of closures reflects a persistent challenge for many small institutions where tuition revenues are declining even as costs continue to increase

## 8.6 Create a Unified Statement

Once your committee has prioritized the needs and benefits for a Lean/continuous improvement approach it's time to draft a unified statement that will be used to explain the "why we are doing this" to all employees.
A simple method I use is to give participants about 3–5 minutes to individually write out possible statements. The statements should be simple, easy to understand, and explain the purpose and intended impact to the institution. When time is up, list all the statements on a whiteboard or flipchart. Have the committee circle the words they like in each statement. Then, have them work together to draft a final statement using those words. Your statement should be shared with others, posted, and used in future communications. Spending time to create the statement is a simple task that can eliminate confusion and reduce variability in communication.

## Reference

ICEF Monitor. 2018. Further Private College Closures Predicted in US (July). http://monitor.icef.com/2018/07/further-private-college-closures-predicted-in-us/.
Kotter, J., Rathgeber, H., 2006. *Our Iceberg Is Melting*. New York: St. Martin's Press.

# Chapter 9

# Planning Your Lean Journey

Once you know *why* you are making the journey it's time to start planning, to put more thought into where you are going and how you plan to get there. Just as in any major effort, planning reduces chaos down the road and increases your chances of success. Most people don't just jump in the car and take off on a cross-country trip without doing some planning. The longer the trip, the more planning that usually takes place. By the same token, most institutions do not kick off major projects or initiatives without a detailed plan. The risks are too high. Lean is not intended to be a limited number of projects with a defined end point. It is a continuous improvement journey. It is on-going, lasting years with the goal of creating a continuous improvement culture. It requires commitment, resources and direction if it is to be successful.

Lean is simply a vehicle to help drive your continuous improvement efforts. Ideally, it is a standard, systematic approach for identifying, evaluating and implementing change. It's important and also daunting to look at the long journey ahead. However, let's keep it simple and focus first on how to get started. Instead of focusing on 3, 5, and 10 year goals, I recommend focusing on just a first year plan. Then, in the spirit of continuous improvement, you would continue to re-evaluate and adjust your plan, your methods, and your goals as you move forward.

In order to begin mapping a route you have to know where you are starting from, your current state or current condition. I'm sure your committee and the institution has a long list of issues each would like to have addressed. You likely have some ideas from the earlier assessment as well. If not, information can be gathered through employee surveys, focus groups, or departmental meetings, and shared with the committee.

## 9.1 Identify and Prioritize Improvement Opportunities

It's time now to start gathering up the low-hanging fruit and figuring out where to start focusing. Earlier I mentioned that during the committee work sessions I educate the group on the common types of wastes. Each waste is defined in detail and several examples are provided.

Another activity that I include in the session is to have the committee break off into subgroups of two to three people. Each group is tasked to discuss and identify where they see inefficiencies or wastes in the current work environment. This activity shifts their thinking away from general negative thinking about problems to focusing in on specific wastes which prevent workers from performing at their best. I like to refer to their wastes as *opportunities* for improvement. Some items may get listed multiple times but it provides a quick picture of a larger range of opportunities. I have each subgroup list their wastes on sticky notes (see Figure 9.1). After about 10 minutes I ask each subgroup to then convert each waste to an action statement (see Table 9.1). In other words, determine what action step or steps need to be taken to address the problem. This again shifts the thinking from the problems to problem-solving. Ask, "If this item was assigned to you

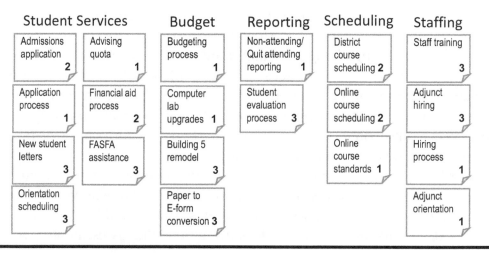

**Figure 9.1  Prioritizing Opportunities**

**Table 9.1  Converting Issues to Action Statements**

| WASTES (Opportunities for Improvement) | POTENTIAL ACTION STATEMENTS |
|---|---|
| Payroll: increase in overtime, number of payroll errors, time it takes to process payroll | Evaluate the payroll process to reduce errors, overtime and improve payroll efficiency.<br>Evaluate the payroll process to reduce the number of errors payroll receives each pay period and the amount of overtime payroll staff spends correcting errors. |
| Student communications: new students receiving multiple letters with confusing or conflicting information, untimely receipt of letters, duplicate letters being sent from different campuses. | Create a continuous improvement team to evaluate the content and timing of new student communications.<br>Review student admissions communications to eliminate confusion to students |
| Staff vacancies: delays in hiring, position approval process | Evaluate and improve the hiring process for fulltime staff. |
| Financial aid: excess motion in processing FASFA applications | Evaluate the FASFA application process to reduce excess motion and improve service to students |

how would you act on it?" Instruct them to make sure that each action statement begins with an action verb. Table 9.1, Converting Issues to Action Statements, is an example of issues being converted to actions. The actions might involve evaluating a process, investigating equipment issues, researching software, conducting time studies, tracking occurrences, conducting observations, or any number of other steps. Don't worry about how large or small in scope the items might be. All problems are wasteful. Some items may be grouped with a larger action, while others could be identified as quick wins and assigned to someone for immediate action. When little problems are taken care of, some of the larger ones diminish or go away.

Next, go around the room and have each subgroup place their sticky notes on the wall and report out their issues and improvement ideas to the larger committee. Allow them time to provide details about their items and short discussions, but don't let it drag on too long. Keep on task and moving forward. This is meant to be a quick sharing of ideas and not a deliberation of all the related problems. If anyone in the group has additional ideas for improvements, have them write those on sticky notes and add them to the wall.

Once all the subgroups have reported out, have the entire committee categorize the items on the wall into common themes. It's likely that you will have duplicate items or several things that could be addressed in one project. For example, you might have several items related to technology training (access, equipment, staffing, materials, and videos) or several issues related to adjuncts (support, resources, training, onboarding). If needed they can rewrite, add to, or combine items as they see fit. Then, have the entire group agree on action statements for each category. It might require several different actions depending on the problem.

Lastly, ask the committee to prioritize the items within each category using a scale of 1–3 (1= high priority, 2= medium priority, and 3= low priority). High priority items should be worked on immediately, medium priority items should be addressed within two to three semesters, and low priority items can be worked on later within the year or delayed until next year.

If the timing is appropriate, have the group take a break while you begin transferring the information to the Leadership Project Planning Register (see Figure 9.2). When the group reconvenes, fill out the remaining categories together. Note, any of the fields in the template can be modified to fit the needs of the organization.

> *Priority* – Priority (1–3) of importance or urgency given to the opportunity or action.
> *Lean opportunity/action* – Lists the actions identified by the group.
> *Strategic alignment* – The strategic goal or initiative the action supports.
> *Start date* –The target day or month you would like the project to start. Priority 2 and 3 item dates can be determined when you are ready to schedule them.
> *Status* – Current status of the project. As you begin launching projects, this is a quick visual to show where each project is in the process. Examples include: on hold, scheduled, in process, implementation, cancelled, complete.
> *Champion* – The leadership person responsible for ensuring the opportunity is acted upon and improvements made.
> *Approach* – The method, tool or approach that will be used for this opportunity. Having your Lean facilitator in the room can help identify approach options. Examples might include focus groups, process mapping, 5S, leadership committee, etc. See more about approaches in the Lean tools section.

**LEAN PROJECT**
8/13/2019

| Priority | Lean Opportunity/Action | Stragegic Alignment | Start date/ month | Status (On Hold, Scheduled, In Process, Implementation, Cancelled, Complete) | C (Champion/ Responsibility) | A (Approach/Method/ Tool) | S (Support/ resources) | T (Team members) | Comments | Suggested Measurements How success of the project will be measured |
|---|---|---|---|---|---|---|---|---|---|---|
| | | | | | | | | | | |
| | | | | | | | | | | |
| | | | | | | | | | | |
| | | | | | | | | | | |
| | | | | | | | | | | |
| | | | | | | | | | | |
| | | | | | | | | | | |
| | | | | | | | | | | |
| | | | | | | | | | | |
| | | | | | | | | | | |
| | | | | | | | | | | |
| | | | | | | | | | | |
| | | | | | | | | | | |

**Figure 9.2  Leadership Project Planning Register**

*Support* – A person or persons who will assist the champion in leading the project. This could include the Lean facilitator, another supervisor/leader or key staff members.

*Team* – Individuals and/or departments that need to be involved. This is an opportunity to begin adding key people that will make up the project team, if they are known. The list does not have to be complete at this time as all participants will later be identified when the project scope is created.

*Comments* – Any additional notes about the opportunity that you want to capture. Examples include: key objectives, issues, barriers, related project information, etc.

*Suggested measurements* – Used to measure project success. This is an opportunity to identify existing or new measurements that can be used to show current performance and future performance of a process. Examples include: cost savings, time savings, error rates, processing time, overtime hours, etc.

Figure 9.2 can be used as a tool for the leadership team to track current opportunities and plan future projects. It should be modified to fit the needs of the organization and can be quickly reviewed in leadership meetings.

# Chapter 10

## Leaders on Board

If you were to ask any organization what key things are needed to be successful at Lean/continuous improvement, it's likely that each would say top leadership support and a good support structure. The purpose of this book is to not only help you launch your Lean initiative, but to also help build your support structure so it doesn't collapse after a few events or when staff changes. The Lean facilitator we discussed earlier is an important part of the structure, but he or she is not solely responsible for ensuring that all changes actually happen. They are the "facilitators" of change. Your leaders are the "leaders" of change and that starts with those at the top. Senior leaders (presidents, vice presidents, president's council, chancellors) are responsible for making big decisions and relying on their direct reports to put plans into actions and carry them out. With regard to Lean this responsibility includes setting the priorities, allocating resources, communicating expectations, and ensuring activities are in alignment with the institution's strategic goals. In addition, each level of the organization plays a key part in the success and/or failure of your Lean initiative. Yes, it is possible to have success applying Lean without senior leader support or within a single department but it will be extremely limited. Each time the changes start effecting other departments who are not also practicing Lean, the efficiencies will stop.

I once asked a college president, "What are your expectations of leaders with regard to Lean?"

He replied, "I expect them all to support Lean."

I countered with, "But what does that look like? What behaviors do you expect from them to show they support Lean? What should they be doing or do differently?"

He simply stated, "They need to support Lean."

His response showed a lack of knowledge about Lean and little thought about how to effectively lead it. The fact that he didn't know was not unusual, it just re-emphasizes the importance of planning what you want to have happen and preparing those who will carry it out.

In this situation I would like to be able to report that steps were taken to clarify the expectations, that desired behaviors were defined, and that top leaders actively showed support for the Lean initiatives by being present and participating in at least a few Lean activities, but I can't. This college has had success in spite of the lack of senior leader support because enough people saw value in it. But, once again, the efficiencies were siloed. When efforts ran up against certain departments that did not have the same vision the efficiencies stopped and frustration grew. The lack of clear expectations allowed certain departments to choose whether to cooperate with change initiatives or not. The failure to address the barriers caused problems between departments and led many to create workarounds, meaning they deviated from standard procedures to avoid the "problem departments." In other cases, major projects sometimes waited years until certain people left, which by the way is counter-intuitive to Lean. I share this with you only in the hope that you can avoid some of these same problems by taking extra steps in the beginning to ensure all your leaders are involved and active in helping to build your Lean support structure.

Let's assume that you yourself are, or have support from, a senior leader who is committed to implementing Lean within your institution. Before we begin discussing steps to building your leader support structure, let me ask a few questions. How do you currently prepare leaders to effectively lead in your institution? Do you have any type of training or standard work steps in place for leaders? My guess is that, like so many other organizations, we do a combination of hiring people with "leadership" experience on their resume, promote someone from within who was good at their job, or as we often do in education, promote individuals based on achieving advanced degrees. We assume these people all have the specific skills we desire.

If you are a leader, how did you learn to become a leader? Ideally you would have had some formal training on best practices, had a chance to practice different skill sets, and maybe were even fortunate enough to have a good mentor that provided guidance and feedback. Unfortunately, most people acquire their leadership skills through on-the-job training, trial and error, and watching the behaviors of others who may not always be good role models. To compound the problem, many leaders often fail to receive timely, constructive feedback about performance unless it is really bad. Numerous studies have shown that the number one reason people leave their jobs is because of their boss, which is very telling, a cause for reflection, and a ripe opportunity for improvement.

Take a moment to reflect on all the leaders you have had in your career. How many leaders have you encountered that were great at coaching and developing their staff, effective at project management, good at problem-solving, and skilled at measuring results? How many were just OK at these things? And lastly, how many were less than okay or substandard? In my 40 years of being in the workforce, I can only recall two supervisors who I felt were truly effective leaders, who helped me to become better personally and/ or professionally. Having been a supervisor in different environments, my training was entirely on-the-job. Most of what I learned about being a supervisor was a direct result of having worked for and around very poor leaders. Instead of witnessing positive leadership behaviors I saw first-hand the negative impact bad leadership can have on staffing, productivity, and worker morale. That type of toxic environment drove me to seek other job opportunities. It's sometimes said that you learn more from bad situations than you do from good. In my case, I learned a great deal about the type of leader *I did not want to be.* I truly hope those of you reading this have had far more positive mentors in your career than I have. I also want to acknowledge that leading people is not easy. It takes practice, training, regular feedback, and knowing what's expected. It's a true skill. It's also about respecting people. Remember, Lean is about helping people to be their best. So how do we help leaders to be their best so they in turn can help their subordinates be their best?

## 10.1 Consider the Culture

Several years ago I attended a national Lean conference. I met with several very knowledgeable Lean practitioners but the one I remember most was a man who worked for General Motors. He was part of a core process improvement team. I recall being impressed by how his company had built their support structure. Their vice presidents were assigned and held accountable for improvement activities within their divisions. Their continuous improvement projects were aligned directly with the strategic plan and their methods for conducting and monitoring continuous improvement events were standardized. But the one thing that puzzled me for quite some time about the continuous improvement practitioner from GM was his comment that "If I don't make someone angry every day, then I'm not doing my job." Having only a few years of formal Lean experience at the time, I struggled with his comment for quite a while, thinking that maybe I was missing something, misinterpreted his comment, or just didn't understand the mysteries of being successful at Lean yet. I've thought about that on different occasions over the years, mainly because it goes against my beliefs of respect for people and collaboration. You know the old saying, "You attract more bees with honey than with vinegar." I prefer to develop collaborative relationships with people. People want to be valued and to be heard. Any basic supervisory class will tell you that. Workers have the job knowledge and your job is to teach them tools that will allow them to create better solutions within their jobs. I know many of you out there are probably in a position similar to mine, in that you have absolutely no positional power to make people do anything. Your power comes from your relationships, building trust, and showing results.

I also want to comment on the power of modeling behaviors. Whether you are aware of it or not, you as a leader set the stage for how people behave and respond to change and to others. The term *leader* infers that others are following, but where are you leading them and do those you lead want to follow you?

I often say that attitude reflects leadership. Not in every instance, but in many. I have conducted over 1500 training sessions and am still amazed at how often I can walk into a group and very quickly distinguish between the different departments and often the type of leaders to whom they report. I recall a Lean training event where my co-trainer and I were facilitating a mapping session for a college on the east coast. We had approximately 18 participants from various departments participating. Prior to the session we were forewarned about the supervisor of the facilities department and his negative attitude. He was not present for the beginning of the training but it didn't take long to recognize those employees in the room who worked for him. Their attitudes were drastically different from other departments represented in the room. Collectively, the facilities department employees were modeling their leader's behaviors and attitudes which were soon validated when he joined us later in the day. The great thing about having strong facilitation skills and the power of the process mapping tool is that during our time together we were able to re-direct those negative and accusatory attitudes into a productive outcome. In fact, the entire group was joking, laughing, and thanking each other for their contributions in the final feedback remarks at the end of the session. Unfortunately, that is not always the case.

On another occasion I worked with a financial aid department whose director was always hostile and accusatory towards anyone questioning her department. So much so that she even accused me of bias in how I set up the mapping event to review the financial aid process. I was following the same standard process that I always use to set up mapping projects. Her behaviors resulted in her staff modeling those same behaviors which were known notoriously throughout the institution. When the director finally retired after several years and a new open-minded person replaced her, the change in attitude was almost immediate.

On a more positive note, I worked with a campus whose leadership transformed its culture from a negative environment for both staff and students to one of acceptance and collaboration. It was easy to transform the physical aspects of the buildings from institution grey and tan to bright colored walls, furniture, and artwork. It took several years of modeling positive behaviors and collaborative work to change the negative environment. Now faculty and staff work collaboratively on everything from budgeting to campus cultural celebrations and more. At the beginning of each semester you will see the campus provost and other staff members greeting students in the hallways, calling many of them by name, and helping to answer questions or provide directions. These leaders lead by example, model the behaviors they desire in others, and celebrate their campus's large diversity in both students and staff.

Be conscious of the type of behavior you want being modeled within your institution. A person's behavior is not always reflective of their leader, but behaviors of a group can be a strong indication of either positive or negative leader modeling. In addition, a leader's behavior can also reflect the behaviors of their senior leader's which can also be positive or negative.

Since we are talking about behaviors and culture, let's address the issue of how exposing problems is handled. A big part of Lean is about identifying wastes, finding ways to remove those wastes, and respecting people in the process. We train people on the wastes so they can identify them. In PM events we use several techniques to identify the wastes and the problems so we can address them. We tell people, "We can't fix problems unless we are aware of them."

I sometimes encounter groups who are fearful or reluctant to discuss their problems. When I use probing questions to try and expose the problems, people minimize the issues or dismiss them as no big deal. Some of this can be due to a lack of training with regard to Lean, but sometimes it's due to the culture, or fear of retaliation or job security. Take a moment and reflect on how you, your department, your campus, and your institution views problems. If asked to give a status update to leadership, do you customarily report more on the good or on the problems you are trying to solve (I like to call these probletunities)? What reaction do you get for reporting positive information? What reaction do you get when reporting issues or things that are not going well? As is customary in our culture, we reward people for reporting good things and often react negatively to feedback that is less than positive. We have been conditioned to only focus on the good and fear the bad. The issue is that hidden problems can grow, causing more to pop up. The avoidance behavior can become infectious until we all go home frazzled and unsure of how much work we actually accomplished that day. If that trend continues you may start to see an exodus from the negative environment, increased absenteeism and declining quality – that is if you measure your quality. But, what if we were all open to discussing problems and truly committed to becoming better? What if we reconditioned our thinking to see problems as opportunities to do better? What would the culture be like then?

I recall an executive director who had a major backlog in the processing of student applications (due to several special circumstances) but was reluctant to share the magnitude of the problem for fear of the negative feedback she would likely receive from leaders above her. Consider whether you have a culture of "hide and seek" – hide the problems and seek only the good – or do you have a culture that is focused on truly making things better. Let's look at a different type of leadership and culture.

Years ago I attended a Lean event where Mike Hoseus spoke. He is co-author of the Shingo award-winning book *Toyota Culture: The Heart and Soul of the Toyota Way*. For close to 20 years he held several positions within Toyota and learned from the Japanese management. He talked in great depth about respecting people and creating a culture where communicating problems is encouraged. What a wonderful approach. Mike told several stories about how Toyota senior management was more interested in problems and what could be learned from them, rather than the things that went well. He shared an experience he had in a Japanese plant where during training for a job on an assembly line he made a mistake and scratched a wheel well. Afraid to tell anyone, but remembering his instructions to pull the andon cord if something went wrong, he hesitantly pulled the cord to signal a problem. Pulling the cord immediately signaled the supervisor. In short, the problem was addressed quickly. Later in a department huddle he heard his name spoken. Not speaking Japanese he knew they were talking about him but didn't know what they were saying. The conditioned expectation of being reprimanded or called out on his mistake lingered. When the meeting was over each worker came by and shook his hand. He later learned through an interpreter that they were thanking him for identifying the problem. If he had tried to hide it, the problem would have passed farther down the line costing more time and resources to fix it at each step.

Picture yourself at any level in each of the above mentioned work cultures. Which environment do you think would be more successful and better at promoting change? Which environment would have a clearer picture of what's really happening?

Being able and willing to identify problems is only part of it. You also have to have a strong support system that can prioritize and act on the issues in a timely manner and communicate what's happening. Ask yourself, what methods can you put in place to create awareness of problems and systematically address them? How can you create an environment where people feel secure in uncovering problems? And going full circle, what kind of behaviors and attitudes do you want modeled within your new culture?

Culture is built over time. It is the result of actions and reactions. It's a product of how people behave and how others respond to those behaviors. Culture can be the result of behaviors being intentionally reinforced or through behaviors being unintentionally reinforced. If you want to build a culture of collaboration within your department or institution people need to have the opportunities to collaborate and be encouraged to do so. If the results of those collaborations are then recognized and rewarded then collaboration becomes part of your culture. If people in your institution are encouraged to bring up ideas and those ideas are valued and rewarded, then sharing ideas becomes a part of your culture. By the same token, if dishonesty and low performance are accepted and unintentionally rewarded (nothing happens to address it), then they also become part of your culture. If you want to change the culture, then encourage, recognize, and reward those behaviors you desire, and in a timely manner discourage or address those behaviors you do not desire.

## 10.2 Building the Support

Creating a continuous improvement culture is not easy and it takes time. It involves being consistent in actions and reactions. It's about building a framework to help support desired behaviors and activities. A key pillar in that framework is your institution's leadership group. They are needed to lead the change process. How well they lead directly impacts how well others follow. Do not assume your leaders will know how to lead or support continuous improvement. Most of them probably have never been exposed to any type of formal Lean or continuous improvement program. Consider what is needed to help them learn about Lean so they can see the benefits and lead their people positively toward becoming Lean advocates and champions. Help them be their best and do their best, so they can help their staff achieve the same.

I've seen situations where top leaders, sometimes having successfully applied Lean at a previous institution, announce that their current institution is going to embark on a Lean journey. Like many new initiatives, a timeline is established, and the next level of leaders is tasked to "make it happen." Each accepts the directive and goes in their separate directions, trying to figure out how to best implement something they likely know little or nothing about in their area, which are often siloed from other areas. They each try to do the right thing, but because the *process* on how to carry it out was not established they experience frustration, confusion, limited success, and the initiative dies a year later. Ironically the very basis of Lean, which includes standardizing processes, minimizing wastes, maximizing efficiency, and developing people, was just thrown out the window in these situations, and they were just getting started.

Take a moment and think about your current leaders. Let's assume they are all trying to do their very best for the institution, their department, and the students they serve. Even with the best of intentions, my guess is that there is a great deal of variation in current leadership behaviors and performance. This is especially true if performance standards have never been identified and your performance review or feedback process is weak.

Be intentional in how you design your support structure. Start by getting all your leaders on the same page and moving in the same direction. If your leaders are expected to support continuous improvement, help them to know exactly what that means, how to do it and why. Take time to align activities and people to create the culture you desire. You will be asking not only your leaders but everyone in the institution to act and behave in a culture that fosters communication, problem-solving, and teamwork. Don't assume they will know what to do. Leaving it to chance invites chaos and more waste. Help them to know what to do and how to do it!

## 10.3 Training Leadership

Start by educating your leadership group on the basics of Lean and why the college/university is planning on doing it. You may not yet have all the details in place but give them an idea of what to expect both in the near future and long term. Include training on change management and refreshers on other supervisory skills such as coaching or situational leadership. Teach them specific behaviors and Lean tools they will use with employees and colleagues to create the desired Lean culture. Allow them time to both practice the skills and collaborate on a unified rollout plan. One or two training classes will not achieve your goal. I often find it ironic that we in higher education are in the business of educating people, but we frequently fail to see the value or commit the time to educate our own employees. Just like your improvement efforts, learning should be continuous. Doing so will help reduce significant NVA during your journey.

Creating your support structure also involves standardizing processes. Standardization helps to reduce variation, errors, and many other types of wastes. It is common to have standard work processes for front-line employees. It is less common to see it applied to leadership, but the trend is quickly growing due to its impact in achieving results. Standardizing leadership activities is referred to as leader standard work (LSW). LSW helps establish baseline expectations for activities that help drive continuous improvement. It helps to align leadership activities, getting everyone to move in the same direction and build on each other's roles. It's a list of repeatable activities that leaders are expected to carry out at specified timeframes (daily, weekly, monthly). LSW is just as important as standard work procedures for front-line staff. It helps reduce variation in how our leaders perform, reduces inefficiencies, and improves service to those they serve. The percentage of LSW activities decreases (Table 10.1) as you move higher in the organization and work activities, by nature of the job, become more variable. However, LSW activities should directly contribute to the goal of helping people perform better in their jobs, improving services, increasing efficiencies, and maximizing resources.

To help you begin aligning your leaders and their activities, we are going to use a popular continuous improvement model called plan-do-check-act (PDCA).

**Table 10.1  Standard Work Percentage**

| Institutional Level | % of Work (Time) that Should be Standard |
|---|---|
| Executive leaders | 10–15 |
| Campus/district | 25 |
| Dept leader/supervisor | 50 |
| Front-line staff | 80 |

PLAN – Think about the characteristics of the culture you want to create. In your leadership training or planning sessions, have the group work collaboratively to identify the characteristics of your desired culture. Then begin identifying activities and behaviors that directly support those characteristics (Table 10.2). Here are steps that can help you get started.

1. Brainstorm characteristics of a Lean/continuous improvement culture on a flipchart, whiteboard, or monitor. Circle those that the group agrees are goals for your institution.
2. List the different organizational levels on separate flipcharts.
3. Under each organizational level, begin listing actions and behaviors needed to support and grow the characteristics identified in #1. Write them as actions (See Table 10.3 Supportive Leader Standard Work).
4. Identify the frequency of the actions (daily, weekly, or monthly).
5. Identify behaviors for each level of the organization that weaken or sabotage the characteristics identified in Step #1 above.
6. Begin with the lowest level of the organization and identify monitoring/accountability steps for each level. Who will monitor whether the agreed-on actions are being carried out? How will it be monitored (form, updates to supervisors, other checks)?
7. Create activities and procedures that quickly address those behaviors that weaken the system (refer to answers for Step #5 above). What happens if a person, area or group routinely fails to perform the agreed-upon actions? What are the consequences? If a leader fails to follow through with one or more actions and there is no corrective action for the behavior, it's like punching holes in the side of a ship. Soon the support structure will weaken, the problem will spread and eventually the Lean ship will struggle to stay afloat.
8. Outline a plan for communicating and implementing the above steps and actions.

The objective of this activity is not to overwhelm people with a whole laundry list of new things to do. It is to *start* building the support structure and support behaviors that drive improvements. If you end up with an expansive list for any of the levels, consider the KISS method (keep it simple stupid). Pick those that are critical but keep them manageable for the people carrying them out. Of course, more details will be needed to

**Table 10.2 Desired Behavior Examples**

| Desired Behaviors | Examples |
|---|---|
| Showing respect for individuals | ■ ask for ideas<br>■ one-on-one coaching<br>■ provide timely feedback<br>■ recognize contributions |
| Meeting and exceeding customer expectations | ■ collaborate with staff to identify exceptional service opportunities and behaviors<br>■ offer/provide customer service training<br>■ recognize employees when they exceed customer expectations<br>■ conduct customer service surveys |
| Encouraging problem-solving | ■ train staff on problem-solving tools<br>■ assign improvement tasks weekly<br>■ regularly solicit improvement ideas and feedback |
| Modeling supportive behaviors | ■ regular coaching of employees on teamwork, problem-solving and other positive behaviors<br>■ demonstrate desired behaviors daily<br>■ be present and available<br>■ involve staff in department improvement and monitoring activities<br>■ work on department issues/improvements<br>■ collaborate with other departments<br>■ track metrics and utilize data to drive progress |
| Developing people | ■ offer/provide staff training on needed and desired topics<br>■ encourage cross-training<br>■ assign staff projects<br>■ recognize team member successes and struggles<br>■ provide coaching<br>■ create opportunities for staff to lead/facilitate improvement activities (training, mapping, meetings, and presentations) |
| Supporting process Improvement | ■ encourage staff input/feedback<br>■ hold frequent but short staff meetings (also known as huddles)<br>■ hold one-on-one coaching sessions with staff<br>■ analyze performance data<br>■ post visual metrics weekly/daily/monthly<br>■ assign improvement tasks<br>■ cross-train employees<br>■ recognize team/individual successes and struggles<br>■ find simple ways to measure performance<br>■ create standard procedures<br>■ address problems in a timely manner<br>■ review/update action items regularly<br>■ provide timely feedback on decisions and changes |

**Table 10.3  Supportive Leader Standard Work**

| Organization Level | Action/Behavior | Frequency |
|---|---|---|
| President | Request project updates at senior leader meetings | Weekly |
| | Request written status updates to share with board of directors | Monthly |
| | Communicate initiatives and celebrate successes at district meetings | Bi-yearly |
| | Address leader/director performance issues | As needed |
| | Work with senior leaders to select district-wide projects | Bi-yearly |
| | Visit departments to show support and gather feedback | Monthly |
| Vice presidents | Outline Lean expectations for the institution | Bi-yearly |
| | Meet with direct reports to align and monitor lean activities, address barriers and secure resources/funding | Monthly |
| | Establish and monitor communication methods (postings, reports, websites, announcements) | Monthly |
| | Work with departments to set performance standards and goals | Yearly |
| | Participate, observe or be present at Lean events | Quarterly |
| | Attend project meetings | Monthly |
| | Address direct report performance issues | As needed |
| Deans/ directors | Hold weekly department meetings, review performance status, request improvement ideas, and assist with problem-solving | Weekly |
| | Post and update improvement ideas and status | Weekly |
| | Provide status updates to Senior Leaders | Monthly |
| | Coach staff in problem-solving tools | Weekly |
| | Establish yearly department performance goals | Yearly |
| Staff | Identify and submit process improvement ideas | Quarterly |
| | Assist in tracking errors | Yearly |
| | Attend a minimum of 2 training events to update skills | Yearly |
| | Work on implementing process improvement ideas | Monthly |
| Faculty | Analyze (program and course) evaluations for improvements | Bi-yearly |
| | Work with program faculty to standardize course content | Yearly |
| | Identify and submit process improvement ideas | Quarterly |
| | Work on implementing process improvement ideas | Monthly |

standardize the process and train everyone. Establish timelines for putting the activities into action.

DO – The next step is to roll out your changes. Assist leaders in practicing and implementing the plan and continue communicating the expectations. Utilize group training sessions where leaders can practice the behaviors and activities before implementing them with their staff. Sessions might include:

- Training on how to design a team board to track improvement activities, communications and metrics
- Training on how to conduct a daily huddle meeting
- Training on how to conduct coaching sessions
- Assistance on how to determine what metrics to gather and how
- Training on process improvement tools
- Training/coaching on change management and situational leadership
- Refining activities and sharing best practices

Tailor the activities to match the area and level of leadership. Build in more feedback and coaching in the beginning until new behaviors become routine. Identify possible support measures or resources to help leaders work through challenges. Determine the type of needed support from the next level of leadership. Your Lean facilitator can be a good resource for some of these activities.

CHECK – Evaluate whether the activities are being carried out and that they are working as intended. Possible methods for checking or monitoring processes include staff evaluations, supervisor observations, check sheets, staff interviews, and frequent "status check" meetings (less than 15 mins) at each level. Determine if adjustments to the plan or activities are needed. Work to standardize the process and the validation steps. These help drive accountability and ensure sabotaging behaviors (identified in the PLAN step) are being addressed in a timely manner. Without them it's hard to hold people accountable. And if people are not performing to the standards, what happens next? This leads us to the next step.

ACT – Determine when a course of action must be taken, the steps to take and by whom. If the plan or the process is not working efficiently, determine the needed adjustments and make them, then re-evaluate. If anyone fails to perform to the minimum standards, what actions are needed to correct the substandard performance? You may already have corrective action steps in place such as creating a personal improvement plan, providing additional coaching sessions, or attending training. How do you ensure countermeasures are timely, both in how quickly they are put in place and how quickly the issue is resolved? What if the substandard performance is from a dean or VP, how is it addressed? If an expectation is found to not align well with the desired behavior, then change it. The goal is to get everyone moving in the same direction, performing in a manner that supports the vision, and correcting behaviors when they start to jeopardize those goals.

Whatever plan you start with will by no means be perfect, but start with some basics and build on it. Young athletes do not become professionals overnight. They start with the basics and then keep adding skills. Serious athletes learn, practice, perform, analyze, and repeat week after week to improve their chances of being successful. Work with your leaders on improving their skill levels. Help them be successful.

During this process of building your support structure it might also be a good time to assess whether you have the right team members in place.

Even after putting all this in place you will still find people who refuse or are reluctant to get on the Lean journey. We call these CAVE people (citizens against virtually everything). Prepare a clear plan for dealing with those people. Ignoring them creates an "infection" that quickly spreads, is hard to cure and can sometimes take years to overcome. Taking even difficult actions shows people that adherence to expectations is important. Work on raising the bar at all levels instead of lowering it to accommodate non-conforming, marginally-productive, and negative staff. Be mindful of the type of culture you want to create.

## Bilbliography

Gallup. 2017. State of the American Workplace. news.gallup.com/reports/199961/7
.aspx?g_source=link_wwwv9&g_campaign=item_236927&g_medium=copy.
Liker, J. K., Hoseus, M. 2008. *Toyota Culture : The Heart and Soul of the Toyota Way*, New York: McGraw-Hill.
Lucas, Suzanne. 2013. Top Reasons People Leave Their Jobs. *MoneyWatch*. October 18. www.cbsnews.com/news/the-top-reason-people-leave-their-jobs/.
Schwantes, M. 2017. Why Are Your Employees Quitting? A Study Says it Comes Down to Any of These 6 Reasons. *Inc.* (October). www.inc.com/marcel-schwantes/why-are-your-employees-quitting-a-study-says-it-comes-down-to-any-of-these-6-reasons.html.

# Chapter 11

# All on Board

The last chapter was intended to help you develop your support plan and implement it, starting with preparing your leaders. Now it's time to plan on how this new focus on process improvement is going to be communicated and rolled out at your institution.

Why do people fear change so much? Mostly because change represents the unknown and it's often thrust upon them with little to no warning and no opportunity to ask questions, provide input or prepare. They become a victim of change and thus do not buy into the proposed changes. As you launch your new Lean initiative try not to make people a victim of change. It's the surest way to anger and alienate the masses. How you prepare people for changes within your institution directly impacts how quickly they support or resist those changes.

Generally, change adoption by employees across organizations follows a natural bell curve (see Figure 11.1). Innovators and early adopters make up 16% of employees, followed by 37% having early majority buy-in, then 37% late majority buy-in, while 16% of employees outright resist change or try to sabotage it (Rogers, 1995).

Consider how you want to introduce your Lean initiative to all faculty and staff. If your first communication will be through a mass email, design it so that it includes the what, why, how, and when, including scheduled times and opportunities to ask questions. Consider holding information sessions, department meetings, all staff meetings, forums, or training sessions to get everyone up to speed and allow them time to ask questions. Educate them on what Lean is and the reasons for doing it. Start building their Lean

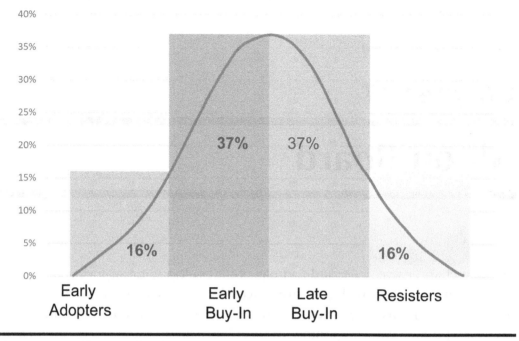

**Figure 11.1    Change Adoption**

vocabulary. Some organizations that I work with schedule a short 2–4 hour Lean overview to do this. The session includes:

- What is Lean and what it is not
- Why the organization has decided to do Lean
- How Lean benefits both employees and the organization
- Review of common types of work wastes
- Overview of two to three Lean tools (those you will be using) to help reduce waste
- A group activity in which participants break into small groups and identify wastes (we like to call them *opportunities for improvement)* they see in their work environment
- Share and discuss the list of wastes/opportunities
- Communicate expectations of employees and what employees can expect over the next few months to one year
- Question and answer period

If your institution is large you might choose to roll out these initiatives one campus, department, or area at a time. For example, if you are a large university, start with selected colleges within the university but have a plan and a timeline for incorporating all others and make the timeline available to everyone at the same time.

Creating various opportunities for people to learn, ask questions, know what's expected, and even get involved can shift the bell curve in your favor. If you remember nothing else, remember to communicate, communicate, and communicate!

# Reference

Rogers, E.M. 1995. *Diffusion of Innovations*, 5th Edition, New York: Free Press.

*Chapter 12*

# Communication

Now might be a good time to also begin developing a communication plan, not just for launching your program but to ensure ongoing communication is intentional and occurring. In all my years of Lean training, communication has always ranked as one of the top areas for improvement in *every* organization. You will not solve the problem of communication but you can be more intentional about what, when, and how information gets distributed.

Technology has offered us an array of platforms to make it easier to communicate: you just have to make sure people know which platforms you will be using and ensure that they have access. Long gone are the monthly reports on green-bar paper or the stapled newsletter. Now we have Share-Point sites, Microsoft Teams sites, webpages, text messaging, e-newsletters, screen pop-ups, display (TV) monitors throughout our hallways, countless apps, and more. You can't pick them all, but decide on a few go-to places where people can "pull" information and also systems or apps that can "push" information on a regular basis without too many manual steps. As you begin to work on projects and implement changes, identify how people will be informed about those changes especially if they are not directly involved with the project. Most colleges/universities who practice Lean have a website that lists their projects. My college recently rolled out a new website, which is actually a SharePoint site where people can submit projects, view current and past projects in detail, view policy and procedure changes, and sign up for push alerts that notify them when something in the category they selected has been added or updated. This is only one method of communication. Microsoft Teams, which is part of Office 365, has recently become popular. It's easy to use and has a variety of functions (notes,

**Table 12.1   Communication Planning Example**

| Tool/ Method | Purpose | Audience | Responsibility | Frequency |
|---|---|---|---|---|
| **Level 1. All employees: *Awareness*. Intended for all levels of employees to communicate information about lean, build basic understanding, and promote lean thinking.** | | | | |
| Presidential email | Awareness of Lean initiatives, results, and direction | All employees | President, Lean staff | Bi-annually |
| All staff presentation | Awareness of lean initiatives, results, direction, success stories | All employees | President, Lean staff | Bi-annually |
| Website | Communicate details on future, current, and past projects | All employees | Lean staff, team sponsors | Monthly |
| Team sites/ team boards | Monitor and communicate department CI/ Lean activities | Department staff | Department leaders | Monthly |
| **Level 2. Leadership: *Awareness and responsibility*. Keep leadership informed of initiatives, requires responsibility on their part to help incorporate changes into work areas.** | | | | |
| Leadership meeting CI/ Lean updates and presentations | Keep leaders informed of each other's projects, promote collaboration, and assess project alignment with college goals | All leaders | Deans/directors, VPs | Monthly |
| Dean/director Meeting updates | Provide awareness of activities and gain support | Deans, directors, provosts, VPs, | Executive VP | Monthly |

(*Continued*)

**Table 12.1    (Cont.)**

| *Tool/ Method* | *Purpose* | *Audience* | *Responsibility* | *Frequency* |
|---|---|---|---|---|
| **Level 3. Senior leadership and governing board:** *Awareness, monitoring, and direction.* **Intended to keep senior decision makers and governing bodies informed to help direct strategic planning activities.** | | | | |
| Senior staff updates | Awareness of Lean activities and outcomes | Senior leaders | President | Quarterly |
| Project report-outs by teams | Provide status updates on current and newly implemented projects | Senior leaders | Project lead | Quarterly |
| Board meeting update | Awareness of lean initiatives and results | Board of trustees | VP, president | Semi-annually |
| Yearly report | Share status of all projects so institutional leaders can monitor progress towards strategic goals | All area leaders, senior staff | Departmental leadership | Annually |

planner, video conferencing, conversations) which allow teams to collaborate all in one space. I actually use it when I'm working with other Lean trainers to share files, have conversations, assign tasks, and conduct video conferences.

Whatever platforms you choose, try to agree on the applications that best fit your needs at that point in time. Technology changes at lightning speed so it's likely you will find better solutions down the road.

To help ensure needed communication is happening at each level take time to prepare a communication plan. An example of what that could look like is shown in Table 12.1.

# Chapter 13

# Preparing to Launch

If you've taken the time to work through the planning activities up to this point, now is the time to start putting all the pieces together to create your first year plan. This plan, much like a roadmap, will help guide your institution through a successful launch and the activities that follow. Remember, failing to plan is planning to fail. Lack of planning evokes chaos and inefficiency. Your plan should be visual and constantly evolving as you do more and learn more. Ideally, it should be referred to frequently as a tool to ensure your institution is on track towards achieving its goals. It is well understood that there is a sharp learning curve for new initiatives so do all you can to develop a plan for a successful launch and first year.

## 13.1 Building Your First Year Calendar

At this point in time your advisory committee (Chapter 7) should have information from prior planning steps and related discussions to start adding activities to your first year continuous improvement calendar. Hopefully, the committee has already begun identifying initial and ongoing training for your leaders. Begin by placing those dates and topics on the calendar. Add in leadership support activities such as coaching sessions or structured checkpoints.

Determine the launch dates and any kick off activities (i.e. meetings, information, and training sessions) for your Lean program and add those to your first year calendar. These are the dates that you will officially kick off your Lean program and communicate what it is, why your institution is doing it, what faculty and staff can expect moving forward, and your expectations. This is where leaders will start using the "why" statement that was agreed upon in Chapter 8. Work backwards from those dates to add key planning steps, communications, program announcements, website launch, and more.

Next, start scheduling continuous improvement projects and activities. Look at the priority opportunities identified by the advisory committee discussed in Chapter 9. From that list pick one or two priority one projects to use as your pilots. Select those that have a high likelihood of success and large potential impact for the college so people will notice and feel the effects of the outcomes. Some of you may have already chosen and conducted pilot projects when you were researching methods early on. However, if you haven't yet conducted pilot projects schedule those now. You may choose to conduct your pilots before officially rolling out the program to the larger institution or after. The benefits of doing them before is that pilot projects are meant to test your methods and people's reactions to the training. You want to put your best foot forward and pilots allow you an opportunity to revise and refine your methods before rolling them out to the larger audience. The outcomes of the pilots can also help sell the program during your launch, assuming the results are favorable. The downside is that people will hear about or be affected by the pilot activities and potentially feel like something is once again being done to them without their knowledge or input. Whether you choose to run your pilots before or after your launch dates, let people know that you are running a pilot and ask them to provide honest feedback for improvement.

Continue planning forward by adding additional priority one projects to your calendar. Refrain from scheduling more than four large projects in a semester for your first year. You will need time to work through the new training process, make adjustments, and establish a repeatable system before going full speed. This will be new for everyone so you will also need to allow for a bit more hand-holding and coaching. Note, project dates may need to be adjusted slightly once the project scopes are completed, but at least you've narrowed down the timeframe. Include checkpoints, project report outs to leaders, senior leader check-ins to monitor implementation of desired behaviors, and advisory committee meetings to your calendar as well. And lastly, include a date at the end of the year to review your process improvement program and make adjustments for the second year.

## 13.2 Preparing Project Scopes

Once you have identified your initial projects, it's time to identify the project lead or point person for each of those projects. You may have already done some of this in the planning session (Chapter 9). If not, do that now. Your Lean/continuous improvement facilitator should contact each project lead to schedule a 1-hour meeting to develop the *project scope* for each initial project. A project scope is a one to two page form that sets up the parameters of the project for both the facilitator and the process owners. At a minimum, the project scope should contain the following elements as seen in Figure 13.1.

## 13.2.1 *Project Statement or Problem Statement*

The project or problem statement is typically one to two sentences describing either what you would like to achieve as a result of doing this project or the problem you are trying to solve. It should include a *what* and a *why*. Examples of such statements are:

- *Streamline the admissions process* (what) *to achieve more timely admission of students* (why)
- *Transition the college from a paper room scheduling process to a district-wide electronic process* (what) *to improve efficiency and service* (why)
- *Standardize the employee off-boarding process* (what) *to minimize security risks, ensure equipment is accounted for, and network files are addressed* (why)

## 13.2.2 *Project Background*

If you are asking people to participate on a process improvement team it's important for them to know the context or background information of why the project was selected and the issues they will be trying to resolve. Include specific problems that exist and any data that might be available. Be careful to state problems objectively to avoid accusing individuals and groups. Blame serves no useful purpose. I find most people try to do their job correctly but when processes are broken even the best workers can look bad.

I have witnessed projects where teams were given a broad topic such as *data*, *work-based learning*, and *customer service* by senior leadership to address institution-wide issues. During an initial 3-hour project meeting teams were expected to develop a project statement that included two to three potential measurements. Because the teams were not supplied with

**Start Date:**
**Target End Date:**

**Project Statement or Problem Statement**
*A brief statement describing what you would like to achieve as a result of doing this project or a problem you would like to solve.*

**Project Background**
*Background information describing the magnitude of the problem, why it needs to be addressed, and why it was selected as a project. Inclusion of data is strongly encouraged.*

**Project Parameters**
*Specify where this project will start and stop (if mapping) or what areas will be included (if organizing spaces).*

**Project Lead(s)**
*Person or persons who will ensure the project moves forward, barriers are addressed and goals are achieved.*

**Project Participants**
*Name, position, department/location*

**Project Goals/Objectives**
*List specific outcomes you hope to achieve from doing this project.*

**Project Metrics**
*List targeted metric outcomes for this project. Make goals specific, measurable, applicable, and time-bound. Example: achieve an error rate on invoices of less than 1% per month.*

**Current Issues/Potential Barriers**
*List current problems. List any potential barriers that could derail the project.*

**Training Schedule**
*Include date, time, location, and whether meals or snacks are provided.*

**Figure 13.1   Project Scope Template**

background information about why the topic was chosen they spent several meetings struggling to simply define their scope. In two instances, when the team finally did agree on a project statement, the college executive vice president made them change their focus because it wasn't what he thought they needed to work on. If the project was important enough to be selected, then all of the issues and problems that made it a priority need to be shared with the team members and the facilitator.

# 13.3 Project Parameters

The project parameters identify specifically what part of the process or what area this project will focus on. If you will be mapping a process, identify what step you will begin with on the map (i.e. application is submitted, new hire is approved, invoice is received) and what step you will end the map with (i.e. student registers for class, new hire completes orientation, invoice is paid). Try to keep the scope narrow to ensure you can complete the project within the allotted timeframe. For example, if your project is to review the hiring process that could involve many different types of hiring (full-time, part-time, faculty, staff, seasonal, student workers, etc.). Pick one, then if time allows, you can always expand it to include other processes.

If your project is to organize a workspace, specify which workspace or workspaces will be included. Below are three different project parameters:

- Department storage areas A and B
- Chemistry lab 104
- Department network drive (if organizing electronic network files)

## 13.3.1 Project Lead

This is the person or persons who are going to lead the implementation of the improvements as determined by the project team. By default this person usually has leadership responsibilities for the process or the department but it can be anyone. For example, the University of Memphis purposely does not assign the process owner (department leader) as the team/project lead. They often have a front-line staff person as the team/project lead. You can also assign co-leaders. The project lead's responsibility is to ensure the project stays on task, status review meetings are held, improvement ideas get assigned, roadblocks are addressed, and implementation is completed. They also ensure project details get communicated to affected stakeholders.

## 13.3.2 *Project Participants*

Project participants are selected based on the project type. If you are conducting a 5S (organizing a workspace) project, for example, then all regular users of that space need to be included. If they are not, those that were absent will not understand what was done and ultimately sabotage the improvements willingly or unwillingly. I once worked with a group of nursing faculty members who eagerly requested help organizing their supply room. It had become a point of frustration so they scheduled a 2-day event with me to work on it. They scheduled it approximately 2 months out to ensure everyone could attend. The day before we were scheduled to begin the project organizer called to inform me that their lab assistant, who I will call Barb, decided at the last minute to take vacation and announced that she had already organized the storeroom. Her attempt at organizing was to rearrange a few things on some shelves and post a few labels and messages not to touch anything.

Barb was responsible for ordering supplies for all the nursing classes for two campuses. She was intentionally invited to participate in the 5S event to help try to get the excessive supplies under control and to help with organization. The group collectively decided to continue as planned with the two-day event without her present. All those in attendance worked well together purging items, organizing supplies by class, setting inventory limits, designing reorder triggers, creating visual instructions, and even collaborated on standardizing supplies to further eliminate excess inventory. They were energized and extremely proud of their accomplishments which no doubt would save the college money and each of them valuable time. Barb came back and within a month completely reversed all the work they had done. Faculty on two different campuses lodged multiple complaints about Barb's behavior regarding this event and other counterproductive actions. It took 2 years before she was finally dismissed, but the damage had been done.

How likely do you think it is that those who attended the 2-day work session will be willing to fully commit themselves to making improvements in the future? The delay in responding to this counterproductive behavior re-emphasizes the need to get leaders on board early, establish expectations for supporting process improvement, and put procedures in place for those that sabotage it.

If you are planning on conducting a PM event, groups of eight to 15 are ideal but it's more important to have the right people in the room. It's imperative that you have at least one representative from each part of the process being reviewed on the team. This should be those who can describe the work steps in detail. There are times when an area leader wants to play that role in place of sending a staff person. Please insist that they have a staff person who does the job in attendance. Leaders need to be involved but cannot take the place of those doing the job. Generally they do not know the job well enough to have the level of detail needed for mapping the steps unless they were recently promoted from that frontline position. If those doing the job are not present to provide specific steps, the group makes assumptions about the steps and their purpose which are almost always incorrect. In addition, those doing the work are key in knowing what needs to be fixed and often how to fix it.

When selecting your participants it is okay to have more than one person representing an area or position. If you do, try to include someone who performs the work really well and one who possibly doesn't. Be careful, however, to avoid anyone who will derail any and all improvement efforts. This includes leadership. If you have a leadership person who is a roadblock it is okay to omit them from the mapping process, though not ideal. Just make sure that their leadership person is in agreement with it. I just had a situation at a college in Michigan where an IT senior leader was purposefully excluded from a mapping event. Two of her staff members, one of whom was leaving the job in 5 weeks, attended as a resource on specific system functions and capabilities. The senior leader questioned why the college would send someone to training who was leaving in 5 weeks. We had to explain that that specific staff person was not receiving training but providing valuable functional details to the project. The senior leader was not invited because of fears she would try to derail the college's second Lean project.

Wouldn't it be nice if we could just be honest and up front with people? Simply say, "You were not asked to be involved for the following reasons." Unfortunately, higher education is horrible at dealing with these kinds of issues. Turnover at most institutions is usually very low partially because people just don't leave. My own institution has an attractive early retirement plan for that very reason. This is one of the main reasons why change in higher education happens at a much slower pace than in private industry.

In an ideal world, sabotaging leaders would receive coaching, be on a performance plan, or be ushered off the bus. However, we do not live in an ideal world so you do what you can and try not to waste everyone else's time. Another example involves one of my early projects with my own college. I was working with a wonderful group of people eager to make the process of students transferring into the college from other colleges/universities easier and more efficient. We made a plan to gather data and found that the average processing time for a student's transcript to be evaluated was 67 days (<1% value added quotient). Unfortunately, the supervisor of admissions and student records at the time was a well-known roadblock. The dean of student affairs and I agreed to only include him in the last session which was when the group would be creating their future state. In hindsight, we should have excluded him from that as well, or better yet, dealt with the behavior early on. The group identified many low/no cost solutions to improving the process and welcomed the opportunity to make changes. However, those efforts fell short of creating and implementing a solid improvement plan because of their leader's negative and blatant sabotaging attitude. I often say that Lean does not fix personnel problems but it does expose them. The supervisor was terminated a few weeks later. However, the damage had already been done. The team was left feeling frustrated because their time and emotional investment into the project resulted in no improvement results.

Another word of caution when selecting participants. There are situations when a key staff person or leader needs to be involved, but for any number of reasons announces they can't attend all the sessions. They ask if they can "step in" to help map their part or show up for just part of the mapping. I want to strongly suggest this *not* be allowed! I have spent my career developing training through trial and error and testing different approaches and methods to see what works best. All participants need to attend all sessions. This is important for many reasons. Those participating in the mapping project over the course of three half-day sessions go from being individuals to becoming part of a team. Throughout the sessions they learn what role each plays in the process, they challenge the process, challenge each other, collaborate on ideas, and share responsibility for the outcomes. Those who "drop in and out" miss all of that and actually hinder the team's ability to effectively evaluate and improve the whole process. It derails it every time. They introduce inefficiencies into the evaluation process because valuable time is spent bringing them up to speed, re-hashing previously discussed topics, re-directing conversations, and trying to answer questions after they leave (because they are no longer present to provide additional information). Someone once said, "It's like they open the door, throw a stink bomb in, then shut the door and leave." I know this sounds harsh but, if someone who needs to be in attendance can't fully commit to the meeting times, change the meeting times or find a different representative.

If your process deals with any type of technology, a technology person who can speak to those systems in your institution needs to be included. This might require having an outside technology expert if the software is new. Make it clear to that person that it is their job to (1) be honest about what technology changes are possible and (2) if a solution is possible, how likely is it to happen. You can waste valuable time and resources by going down a technological path that is possible but not likely to happen. In addition, you don't want to task the IT department, which usually has a backlog of projects, with unrealistic expectations or work that hasn't been properly vetted. In some cases, I've seen technology requests from Lean projects get assigned a higher priority because of the fact that the requests have been properly vetted and agreed upon by cross-functional representatives.

Remember, Lean is about creating value for the customer. When evaluating processes always try to include your customer. Each person who has a part in the process is a customer of the previous person in the process. But, whenever possible, include an *end customer*. An end customer is someone who is the recipient of the final product or service. This could be a student, parent, vendor, company, faculty member, a department, or other group. It may not always be possible, perhaps due to confidentiality reasons, but know that when possible they can provide important insight into how the process is really working and what's of value to them as a customer. If they are external to the college I would consider asking them anyway. Some are eager to participate in the hope it will improve what they experienced or just for the experience of seeing how process improvement is done.

### 13.3.3 Project Goals/Objectives

As you consider a project, identify what you hope to achieve as a result of conducting this improvement activity. Is it cost savings, time savings, better communication, cross training, process understanding, or better customer service? You are asking people to take time away from their already busy schedules so make sure you know what outcomes you are hoping to achieve. I had a company manager once fill out the scope and send it back to me prior to our scheduled conference call. During our conference call I started walking through his goal statements which were very vague and broad. Basically they sounded good on paper but provided no substance.

They included things like better communication, customer accountability, and improved profitability. When I asked him to explain exactly what he meant by some of the statements as it pertained to this project he found it difficult to come up with any answers. He treated the document as just another form he had to fill out to get started. If the person setting up the project doesn't know what they want to achieve you run the risk of not inviting the right people to the project or floundering with the direction you want it to take. As a facilitator leading a project, I rely on clear objectives to know where to lead the group and to know what I have to help them to achieve. In the case of the manager, he quickly apologized and said, "I think I need to go back and really think about what I want from this."

Try to create objectives that are detailed, specific, and can be understood by all involved. Shoot for a minimum of five good objectives. Avoid making statements that include more than one objective. For example, the following contains two objectives: *reduce the amount of copying and manual signatures required*. When the project is complete and it's time to evaluate whether the objectives were met, you want to be able to say "yes, we achieved that" or "no, we did not achieve that." In the example statement you may have reduced the copying but not the signatures so it's not an easy yes/no question.

Once you've identified your objectives, now it's time to determine what can be measured.

## 13.3.4 Project Metrics

The next step is to look at the objectives that you just wrote and try to determine if there is a way to quantify or measure them. How would you be able to "show" that the objective was achieved? Not all objectives will be quantitative but try to include ones that are. If you struggle with this, don't hesitate to solicit help from resources within the institution who like working with numbers and reporting.

If possible, try to create SMART objectives. SMART stands for specific, measureable, achievable, realistic, and time-bound. Some examples of SMART objectives might be:

Objective: Ensure all purchases are properly approved before purchasing
SMART Objective: Reduce the number of confirming POs after the purchase is made by 73% by May 30th
Objective: Ensure accuracy of information between departments

SMART Objective: Reduce the number of errors, including missing or
  illegible information, received by registration by 30% within 3 months
Objective: Automate approvals
SMART Objective: Eliminate the need for manual signatures by July 1st
Objective: Reduce payroll errors
SMART Objective: Reduce the number of payroll errors per pay period by
  25% by the end of the fiscal year
Objective: Improve student acceptance communications
SMART Objective: Reduce the average lead time for student acceptance
  communications from ten days to three days by January 15th

Why collect metrics? Metrics have the ability to show us where we've been,
where we currently stand and where we are in relation to our goals. They
have the potential to provide critical information about the health of our
processes and our business activities.

Consider the dashboard of your car. You have a speedometer that shows
when you're going too fast, a gas gauge that warns you to fill up before
running out and other indicator lights (oil, engine, temperature) that alert
you to take action before things really get bad. Imagine taking a long road
trip through cities, mountains, deserts in all types of weather without any
form of dashboard displays or mirrors in your vehicle. In addition, let's
pretend you have no map (strategic plan) or GPS to guide you and you've
only allocated a small budget for the trip. How well do you think your trip
would go? How pleasurable (or stressful) would it be and how efficiently
would you arrive at your destination? What types of problems could potentially become major barriers or roadblocks if they were ignored or went
unnoticed? Metrics help inform us of when to take action, make adjustments,
and also help validate when things are running well.

I will tell you that the metrics section is the most difficult part of the
project scope to complete. Sometimes it's difficult to know what metrics to
collect until you get into the details of the project. Whether you determine
your metrics prior to starting your project or during it, I urge you not to
overlook their importance.

I once worked with a large city government on a project to improve their
vehicle maintenance process for their city fleet. It was a very large project that
eventually resulted in significant improvements and cost savings for the city.
My co-trainer and I led the group through mapping of their project and
creation of an implementation plan. During that time we pushed the team to
gather metrics and offered many suggestions on possible data points. Our

involvement with the team ended one month after the training as we moved on to help initiate other projects within the city. The team continued to implement their improvement plan. When the project ended, the team was asked to present their project to the city council. Since we were still involved with multiple projects with the city, I decided to attend the meeting to hear their results. The entire team attended the report with one spokesperson designated to report on the details of their project. It was very informative and going very well, up to the point where a council member asked for measure-able outcomes. He wanted to know how much better the process was and if there were any cost savings to the city. The entire energy of the room changed as the spokesperson announced that the group chose not to collect that type of data. Being fairly knowledgeable of the project, I knew their improvements were significant but they had no way of "showing" that to the council. It went from being a very high energy, celebratory report to falling flat and failing to get the team the recognition they deserved. I followed up with the department director a few months later. He and his team did eventually manage to gather data to show significant efficiencies and cost savings but the council opportu-nity was already lost. Their success was later highlighted in *Government Fleet* (Basich, 2011).

As you scope out your project, try to find data that will help tell your story both now and in the future. Think about the problems you are trying to address and how you will show whether things are improving or not. Metrics can be tracked just through the end of the implementation phase (to verify changes worked) or long term (as a business monitoring tool). Because it is difficult to try and determine what types of data to collect, I often share a list like the one below to help spark ideas.

- Conversion rate
- Cost
- Customer ratings or complaints
- Frequency
- Lead time
- Number of approvals (electronic)
- Number of copies made
- Number of databases/systems used
- Number of errors/edits/return rate
- Number of hand-offs
- Number of initial entry points to the process
- Number of manual steps

- Number of people item passes through
- Number of signatures (manual)
- Overtime hours
- Processing time
- Quantity
- Quality
- Survey ratings
- Time

To be effective, metrics must be easy to collect, timely, easy to interpret, and controllable. It's important to gather data *before* any changes are made to give you a baseline or starting point. Once you've identified the metric, determine how it will be collected, by whom, and for what time period. If you already have historical data you can pull from, your job just got easier. Maybe there are already reports being generated that you can use or make a few modifications to in lieu of collecting data manually. If nothing yet exists, don't ask people to spend large amounts of time to manually collect and process data. Instead, try finding simple methods of collecting measurements that are project specific and for a shorter time period (i.e. samplings). Maybe collect data for 2 weeks or 1 week a month instead of everyday for 6 months. I've had groups conduct surveys, use tracking sheets, tick sheets, and conduct time studies to collect data that wasn't readily available. For example, if errors are one of your metrics and they aren't currently being tracked, work with the group to establish a simple tick sheet (Figure 13.2) with the most common error types. Agree on the method and time period for recording the errors. Each time a person encounters an error they simply make a mark under the corresponding error type. The second example (Figure 13.3) is a tracking sheet and requires people to provide a bit more

| Staff Person | Missing Data | Incorrect Data | Incorrect Quantity | Budget Issue | Duplicate Submission |
|---|---|---|---|---|---|
| Jacki | IIII | II | | II | ЖЛ |
| Elliot | ЖЛ | II | I | I | ЖЛ ЖЛ II |
| Pam | ЖЛ ЖЛ I | III | II | I | ЖЛ III |
| TOTAL | 20 | 7 | 3 | 4 | 25 |

**Figure 13.2   Tick Sheet: March Purchase Request Errors**

| Contact Name | Date | Time In | Process (10 words or less) | Date | Time Out |
|---|---|---|---|---|---|
| John Stuart | 4/13 | 8:20 AM | Open mail and post to SIS | 4/13 | 8:25 AM |
| Martha Meyers | 4/15 | 10:52 AM | Prepare cover sheet for evaluation | 4/15 | 11:00 AM |
| Teresa Mosher | 4/16 | 7:30 AM | Date stamp, run GAR and file | 4/16 | 7:45 AM |
| Peter Rosko | 4/19 | 1:08 PM | Evaluate transcript | 4/24 | 2:15 PM |

**Figure 13.3   Tracking Sheet: Transcript Evaluation**

information. For example they might need to record the task or action performed and processing time.

The results of your data can help to show where your largest issues and opportunities exist, making it easy to prioritize the work. It's great when you can identify metrics that have long term value, those that can help drive performance and provide the "warning signals" for when adjustments are needed.

For example, a college payroll department tracked payroll errors for up to 2 years beyond their implementation phase. Information from their tracking allowed them to continue to improve their staff training and communication and drove programming changes that eventually eliminated the manual tracking steps. Other project metrics that became long term included tracking waiting times for counseling and advising appointments, tracking student volume per advisor, and overall department volume. The data helped leaders determine when adjustments needed to be made to staffing levels, processes and planning.

An important note to remember when determining long term metrics is that what gets measured and what gets rewarded influences how people work. As an example of ineffective metrics, let's imagine you want to set a metric for your student recruitment office. You want to make sure that your recruiters are making contact with as many prospective students as possible in order to increase admission numbers and, in turn, enrollment. So the decision is made to track recruiter contacts by monitoring the number of inquiry forms they receive from prospective students. The recruiter's focus is now on how to collect the most inquiry forms. They may do things like offer a prize for filling out a form, ask people to fill out a form who are not interested in going to college, or some other gimmick just to get the completed inquiry form. Because the metric was just on the number of forms, chances are that many of the forms are not even from prospective students making them meaningless. On the other hand, what if instead they had tracked the number of prospective students that actually signed up for orientation or completed an application? More time might be invested in who the recruiters talk to and how well they follow up on those inquiries.

Some examples of poor metrics include tracking the number of continuous improvement projects but failing to track the results of those projects, or tracking the number of business client visits without tracking the number of different clients who actually purchase training.

More positive examples of good metrics include: an admissions department measuring the number of applications that result in registrations; a contract training department measuring the number of new client training events; a facilities department measuring the number of successfully completed work orders by month, trade, and customer feedback.

As you think about your project and the eventual implementation phase, consider not only the short term metrics that show whether your outcomes were successful, but also what long term metrics would be beneficial for monitoring on-going conditions and making informed business decisions.

## 13.3.5 Current Issues and Potential Barriers

Something else I like to include in my project scope is a section that will inform me, as a facilitator, of the current issues and potential barriers that exist with the project. When I sit down with a department leader or process owner I listen to their complaints, frustrations, and main reasons for wanting to work on this project. I note them in this section and use the information to validate that their goal statements are addressing the right problems.

I also use this section as an opportunity to identify any hidden barriers that could potentially derail or detour the project. Sometimes we like to refer to such items as "the elephant in the room." This is the big barrier that everyone knows is a problem but doesn't want to talk about, hasn't wanted to address, or has been unsuccessful at addressing. Sometimes this is a person or a department's behavior, practices, or some past event that continues to cause problems. An example I encountered was outdated software and no money to replace it. It may be software that was recently purchased but is not working as intended and replacing it is not an option. Whatever it is, the facilitator needs to know what they are dealing with and the magnitude of the problem. For example, if it is a leader who is likely to block everything then Lean is not going to solve it, and other courses of action need to be recommended. If the barriers have more to do with personality differences, lack of understanding, reluctance, or differing viewpoints, then I specifically ask if there is anything I need to know or that needs to be discussed. As a neutral party it's often easier for me to play dumb and ask the obvious questions than it is for people involved in the problem. If the issue is a person or department or it's sensitive in nature, you may choose to document it on the project scope but redact it on the version that is sent out to participants.

## 13.3.6 *Training Schedule*

The final section in the project scope is the training schedule. If at all possible try to establish training dates at the same time you are drafting the rest of the project details. This eliminates a lot of back and forth and delays in getting your project started. If firm dates cannot be scheduled at that time, at least identify potential dates or agree on a timeline for checking schedules and confirming dates. If it's of value, you may want to include a target completion date for the project. This date indicates when you want implementation to be completed and a report of the outcomes given to key leaders. This sometimes helps ensure implementation is timely and doesn't get drawn out too long. A good timeline is 3–6 months for projects that don't involve buying and implementing new software which can sometimes take up to a year.

Your project scope is a living document, meaning that it should be updated to reflect any changes. I use a project scope for setting up all types of improvement projects, not just mapping. As a facilitator, I use the project scope as a:

- guide to know what I need to achieve during the event
- communication tool to inform participants about the project they will be participating in
- summary to leaders about the project
- reporting tool following implementation

Some institutions may choose to use a project charter to define their improvement project instead of a project scope. Though there are differing opinions about their differences, I view a scope document as being more of a tool for the facilitator and the project group. In contrast, a project charter contains the project scope along with additional information that is important to senior leadership. The additional components can include an estimated budget, projected return on investment (ROI), constraints, milestones, timelines, sponsors, and risks. Charters usually require approval by key leaders before projects are allowed to begin.

## Reference

Basich, G. 2011. Ankeny Overhauls Fleet Maintenance Procedures to Improve PM and Availability. *Government Fleet*, August 8, 2011. www.government-fleet.com/75266/ankeny-overhauls-fleet-maintenance-procecures-to-improve-pm-vehicle-availability.

# Chapter 14

# Planning Considerations

When colleges first begin focusing on formal process improvement projects there are usually a plethora of large cross-functional projects to select
from. I recommend selecting only four to six large-scale cross-functional
projects per year. Having more than that negatively affects the quality and
completeness of implementation. Focus on implementing positive change
rather than on the number of projects. I worked with an executive vice
president who after 2 months on the job kicked off five large-scale district
projects. After 10 weeks of combined training and team work sessions,
each project group reported out their recommendations for improvements
to senior college leaders. The report-outs were celebrated with plaques for
all participating team members but nothing had yet been implemented.
A year later several of the teams were still working to implement their plan
and achieve tangible improvements. Five months after the first groups
reported out to leaders, six more district teams were launched and another
four teams 5 months after that with similar results. Unfortunately the focus
of this program was on the report-outs and less on actually implementing
changes. It's important to note that the longer a project is "in process" the
greater the cost (staff time) and the less that gets implemented. People
also have to see and feel change happening and feel positive results in
order to remain motivated. Another downfall is that no time was allotted
to assess how the continuous improvement process itself was working or
not working. Remember, it's NVA activity unless you can make positive
change happen!

In addition to focusing on results, try not to focus on just one type of
result. I had an organization once that would only approve projects if the

estimated cost savings met or exceeded a certain dollar threshold. Because the organization was so heavily focused on the cost savings, many smaller projects that could collectively have led to significant cost savings, time savings, and improved service were overlooked. In addition, the Lean practitioners were forced to spend significant amounts of their time evaluating costs and calculating savings causing them to spend less time working with groups to implement change. Remember that little changes add up to big changes.

Other things to consider as you build your first year schedule:

■ Limit the number of Lean tools you start with. Many colleges start with process mapping and 5S (organizing workspaces). Get good at using those two tools, standardize their delivery, and then add in other tools as needed.
■ Include your Lean trainer/facilitator in the scheduling process. If you are using an internal (on staff) trainer/facilitator, determine if they need training or developmental time to prepare. If utilizing external Lean consultants set up a meeting with them to work out an appropriate schedule.
■ Be conscious of key people and the extent of their workloads. Try to choose projects in different areas or with different focuses so that key individuals don't get pulled into more than one major project at a time. Remember, they still have their everyday responsibilities to attend to.
■ Try to incorporate different people rather than always using the same few from a department, site or area. The goal is to eventually get everyone involved in process improvement. When more people become familiar with Lean and see positive results that's when the culture changes.
■ Try to avoid busy times for involved departments such as the beginning of the semester for student related services, beginning and end of semester for faculty or end of fiscal year for business/financial services. Work with participants to find optimal meeting times and schedules.

Continue to add to and make adjustments to your first year calendar. Include key communication dates, scheduled project report-outs, and status updates. Consider adding formal accountability check points throughout the year and include people responsible for the activity. For example, part of the president's responsibility in our earlier example (Table 10.3 Supportive Leader Standard Work) was to request project updates weekly. Those updates might be less formal but you may also consider scheduling a specific meeting time dedicated to more formal project updates, maybe once a quarter or semester.

Other dates to include on your calendar might be strategic planning meetings and dates on which the next round of projects will be selected and started. One institution that I reviewed for accreditation used an all-staff day that was dedicated to discussing and identifying process improvement opportunities. Ideas were submitted and a review committee evaluated each based on specific criteria (budget, student impact, cost savings, etc.). Those that met the criteria were prioritized and received funding/support for that year. This might be something to add to your yearly calendar down the road, once you have your continuous improvement system established.

## Chapter 15

# Working Your First Year Plan

If you have followed the steps listed in this book up to this point, you should have a solid start to begin creating your first year plan. Your plan (or calendar) is a working document that shows your continuous improvement activities and other activities that support your Lean initiatives throughout the year. Your plan should be constantly updated as new information becomes available. Placing dates on the calendar, assigning responsibility, monitoring progress, and working the plan will help launch Lean in your institution. Remember, failing to plan is planning to fail. The first year is a learning experience so try not to overdo it by scheduling too many activities or being unrealistic with timelines. Use lessons learned in your first year to assist you in your second year planning. There will be many challenges in this uncharted journey but stay the course and communicate like crazy. Keep people informed about what activities are taking place, changes that will impact their jobs, results being achieved, and expectations for them moving forward.

As you work through the activities in your plan (trainings, communications, monitoring, etc.) identify repeatable patterns. Begin standardizing your approach, how you identify projects, how you schedule projects, how you communicate information, what you communicate, how you conduct training, and how you monitor progress. We touched on the popular PDCA cycle in Chapter 10. It's a cycle of repeatable steps to help standardize your improvement process. A lack of standardization, as you saw earlier in the discussion of wastes, creates chaos and inefficiency. Many important processes (budgeting, billing, strategic planning, accreditation, etc.) have recurring cycles that contain elements of planning, implementation, evaluation, and adjustments. Your process improvement cycle should not be any different. Each time you conduct a training or activity, plan for it, do it, study or evaluate the outcomes, and then make adjustments to improve it the next time. My co-trainers and I always evaluate each and every training session or event to determine what went well, what needs improvement, and how we want to improve it before we deliver it again. I've been doing some of the same trainings for almost 20 years and we are still finding things to improve. It is important for continuous improvement practitioners to improve their own processes. As my fellow practitioner, Stephen Yorkstone of Edinburgh Napier University said, "Eat your own dog food. Do Lean in a Lean way. Use the tools on yourself. Keep running experiments" (Yorkstone, 2018).

When you approach the end of your first year, honor the cycle of continuous improvement (PDCA) and collect feedback from project groups, staff, faculty, and leaders on your continuous improvement program. What are your successes and opportunities for improvement? Hopefully you've been making adjustments along the way, but now is the time to step it up and plan for the next year. Dedicate time on your calendar to hold a continuous improvement review and planning session(s) with leaders. This review portion could include:

■ Methods and tools – What worked well and what improvements are needed?
■ Resources (money, staff, materials, etc.) – What adjustments are needed?
■ Support structure – Where is support lacking? What activities, behaviors and practices are working well? What changes are needed? What new ideas should be introduced?

The planning portion could include:

■ New project identification and prioritization
■ New and continued Lean training to maintain and enhance Lean knowledge and skills
■ Second year calendar planning

# Reference

Yorkstone, S. 2018. Lean Book [Email].

# Chapter 16

# Conclusion

This book has laid out multiple factors affecting the future of institutions of higher education and provided critical planning steps. It seems apparent with what is happening in the current educational environment that the status quo is no longer enough to guarantee a viable existence for colleges and universities. The choice then becomes to look for solutions, and change the ways of doing business now so as to not only survive but thrive. Failure to do so risks decline and extinction. You are sure to encounter obstacles beyond your control, whether it be timing, financial resources, leadership structure, level of senior leader support, or any number of other barriers. Despite the obstacles, I encourage you to keep moving forward with your efforts.

Lean has a proven track record in manufacturing, industry, and higher education for reducing costs and simplifying processes which saves time, energy, and resources that can be allocated elsewhere. In addition to improving quality, Lean also leads to more productive, engaged, and satisfied employees as well as customers, who in this case are the students. Lean has now been utilized within the higher educational setting and has proven to be very effective, as you can see from examples listed in this book.

The information in this book has provided you with what Lean is, how to get started, and ideas on implementation. Hopefully it will help you to get your institution started on a Lean journey now. Feel free to contact the author at bonnieslyk@gmail.com.

# Index

Page numbers in *italics* refer to information in figures/diagrams; those in **bold** refer to tables.